Emotion Coaching with Children and Young People in Schools

of related interest

The Incredible Teenage Brain
Everything You Need to Know to
Unlock Your Teen's Potential
Bettina Hohnen, Jane Gilmour and Tara Murphy
Foreword by Sarah Jayne Blakemore
Illustrations by Douglas Broadley
ISBN 978 1 78592 557 3
eISBN 978 1 78450 952 1

Being Me (and Loving It)
Stories and activities to help build self-esteem, confidence,
positive body image and resilience in children
Naomi Richards and Julia Hague
ISBN 978 1 84905 713 4
eISBN 978 1 78450 236 2

**Building Happiness, Resilience and
Motivation in Adolescents**
A Positive Psychology Curriculum for Well-Being
Ruth MacConville and Tina Rae
ISBN 978 1 84905 261 0
eISBN 978 0 85700 548 9

Life Coaching for Kids
A Practical Manual to Coach Children and Young
People to Success, Well-being and Fulfilment
Nikki Giant
ISBN 978 1 84905 982 4
eISBN 978 0 85700 884 8

**Attachment and Emotional
Development in the Classroom**
Theory and Practice
Edited by David Colley and Paul Cooper
Foreword by Barry Carpenter
ISBN 978 1 78592 134 6
eISBN 978 1 78450 399 4

Emotion Coaching with Children and Young People in Schools

Promoting Positive Behavior, Wellbeing and Resilience

Louise Gilbert, Licette Gus and Janet Rose

Foreword by John Gottman, Ph.D.

Jessica Kingsley Publishers
London and Philadelphia

First published in Great Britain in 2021 by Jessica Kingsley Publishers
An Hachette Company

2

Copyright © Louise Gilbert, Licette Gus and Janet Rose 2021
Illustrations copyright © ECUK 2021
Foreword copyright © John Gottman, Ph.D. 2021

The right of Louise Gilbert, Licette Gus and Janet Rose to be
identified as the Author of the Work has been asserted by them in
accordance with the Copyright, Designs and Patents Act 1988.

Front cover image source: Emotion Coaching UK.

A CIP catalogue record for this title is available from the
British Library and the Library of Congress

ISBN 978 1 78775 798 1
eISBN 978 1 78775 799 8

Printed and bound in the United States by Integrated Books International

Jessica Kingsley Publishers' policy is to use papers that are natural,
renewable and recyclable products and made from wood grown in
sustainable forests. The logging and manufacturing processes are expected
to conform to the environmental regulations of the country of origin.

Jessica Kingsley Publishers
Carmelite House
50 Victoria Embankment
London EC4Y 0DZ

www.jkp.com

Contents

Figures and Tables

Acknowledgements

Our first thanks must go to John Gottman and his colleagues who inspired us to start our own Emotion Coaching journey and led us to write this book. We'd also like to express our deepest gratitude to all the practitioners and parents who have participated in our research over the past ten years, sharing their stories, experiences and challenges, which have enriched and deepened our understanding of Emotion Coaching and how it translates to the professional world of practice. We're especially grateful to Felicia Wood for her contributions to this book and to the many Emotion Coaching UK (ECUK) practitioner trainers who have kindly given permission to feature some of their stories about using Emotion Coaching. A big thank you also goes to Katrina Rose for her wonderful illustrations. And finally, we'd like to express our admiration for all the children and young people who have worked with us and the many practitioners to promote positive behavior, wellbeing and resilience in the classroom.

Foreword

This is a great book. I am delighted to be asked to write a foreword for it because it will help children and the adults who care about them have much more satisfying and longer lives.

The fact is that many children throughout the world feel alone and unsupported, and they often encounter a barrage of adult expectations, adult disappointments and adult criticisms. It is common that children feel no one understands them or the everyday world they live in. They also feel powerless to have any impact on their own lives. They didn't create this world, but they're expected to adapt to it and to be grateful to us adults that they get to be in it at all.

To open a powerful connection with a child, emotional moments offer precisely the window we need to understand the child's world. When I do talks for parents, they usually want to know what they ought to TELL children, whereas I emphasize that they need instead to LISTEN to children. Surprisingly, they want to know how exactly they can accomplish that. Emotion coaching is how to accomplish great listening to children.

In talks I've given, I've asked audiences whether anyone remembers what it actually felt like to be a child. Only a proportion of hands go up. I then ask those who can recall whether there was an adult they remember who communicated that they liked them, even loved them, supported them and listened to them. Only a few hands remain up. I then invite those people to tell a story to the group about that adult. The stories they share are invariably moving, and they talk about these rare adults with tears of gratitude. The moments they share were powerful and rare events in these people's lives as children. But this kind of emotional connection with a child does not have to be rare. Parents and teachers can become allies of a child if they learn to do emotion coaching, if they learn to listen, empathize and also set fair limits on misbehavior, and only from that context of acceptance do mutual problem-solving with a child.

Emotion coaching has been shown scientifically to be highly effective in the US by our lab, in Australia by Sophie Havighurst, in South Korea by Christina Choi and now by this stalwart group of authors in the UK. Amazingly, everywhere on the planet kids need to be seen by the important adults in their lives. They yearn for understanding and emotional connection. Kids *all* over the world are really—in a very important way—very much the same.

Not only do kids yearn for this kind of connection with adults, but, as this wonderful book shows, they also benefit enormously. Emotion coaching teaches children to trust their own feelings. Kids who are emotion coached learn that their emotions are their GPS in life. When they're angry they learn that there's a goal they have that is being blocked. When they're sad they learn that something important is missing in their lives. When they're afraid they know to create safety. They learn to listen to their own feelings. Gavin deBecker's book *The Gift of Fear* shows dramatically how listening to our own fear is the only way to stay safe. Staying safe doesn't happen when people carry guns or learn karate. It happens when we follow our natural intuitions. Listening to and trusting all our own emotions provides us with a guide to knowing if that job, or that relationship or that place we live in is wrong for us. We can then act with our own emotions as part of our life compass. Emotion coaching changes us as individuals.

Emotion coaching also changes our relationships with others. The co-regulation of emotions that the authors of this mighty book teach with emotion coaching leads to SELF regulation in children. Self-regulation skills actually physically change the brain and the entire peripheral nervous system, including the powerful vagus nerve. Self-regulation then makes it easier for children to focus attention, to become resilient in the face of everyday stresses, to self-soothe, to stay healthy and to achieve up to their full potential. It also teaches children lifelong *emotional intelligence*, which has a profound impact on their own social skills with other kids. They not only learn to listen to their own feelings. They develop the skills to become a good friend, to develop strong relationships with others. Emotion coaching also changes the adults who practise it. It opens their world in ways they cannot even imagine, because the emotions convert a grey, dull world into a world that exists in living, dramatic technicolor.

The data is very clear. The benefits of emotion coaching to children and adults are enormous. And so, emotion coaching needs to become a part of every adult's skill set. Not only because of its many benefits to both adults and children. It also needs to become a part of every adult's skill set because it's so much fun to do, and it provides a way to better love one another. So, learn emotion coaching to give more love to others, and you will receive more love as well.

John Gottman, Ph.D.
Orcas Island, WA

Introduction

Our research tells a simple but powerful story about how Emotion Coaching has been successfully introduced as a novel approach to support children's behavioral regulation in educational and community settings (Gilbert, 2018; Gus *et al.*, 2017; Rose, McGuire-Snieckus and Gilbert, 2015). All the research on Emotion Coaching, including our own studies, suggest that it is a credible, evidence-informed approach suitable for use in professional practice and settings.

Resilience and wellbeing are linked to better general health, life expectancy, educational outcomes, engagement in healthier lifestyles, productivity at work and stronger social relationships. Historically, factors such as wellbeing and resilience were not considered necessary for educational attainment. However, they are now recognized as integral to educational success (Durlak *et al.*, 2011; Feinstein, 2015). Research now suggests that social and emotional intelligence, of which our ability to regulate our emotions is an integral part, profoundly affects learning, attention, memory, decision-making and social functioning (Goleman, 2007; Gross, 2015; Shonkoff and Garner, 2012). Indeed, Immordino-Yang and Damasio (2007, p.3) claim, "neurobiological evidence suggests that the aspects of cognition that we recruit most heavily in schools, namely learning, attention, memory, decision making, and social functioning, are both profoundly affected by and subsumed within the processes of emotion."

Therefore, it is important that today's children, who will be tomorrow's society, have the skills and knowledge to understand that we all have emotions and they are natural and normal. They need to recognize emotions in themselves and others and in doing so manage emotions more effectively to problem-solve and engage with others.

Emotion Coaching supports children to develop emotion regulation skills that will help not hinder their engagement in life-long learning. The term "Emotion Coaching" was created by US psychologist Dr. John Gottman and his colleagues (Gottman, Katz and Hooven, 1997) to describe a natural parenting strategy they observed while researching family relationships. Gottman identified that the children of parents who used Emotion Coaching had better health, more positive social relationships, higher academic achievement, improved behavior and greater resilience.

This book provides a practical guide to Emotion Coaching, an evidence-based approach and technique for supporting children and young people to develop better self-regulation, improve their behavior and enhance their wellbeing and resilience. Emotion Coaching has become widely used in educational and community settings (as well as the home) throughout the UK and beyond. It provides practitioners with an accessible tool and framework for helping children and young people to regulate their feelings and behavior. The book promotes two key messages: that "relationships matter" and that "emotions matter to learning."

Chapter 1 provides a clear rationale for practitioners to justify the use of Emotion Coaching in their classrooms. It introduces the idea that emotions are universal and inform all behaviors. There is a brief overview of some of the emerging research suggesting how behavioral responses arise and affect our wellbeing and resilience.

This focuses on the processes by which Emotion Coaching appears to support children's ability to self-regulate.

Chapter 2 traces the origins of Emotion Coaching as a parenting style and outlines the various processes that comprise Emotion Coaching as identified by Gottman and his colleagues. It then describes how these processes can be translated into four identifiable steps, based on our research. It considers the different ways in which adults approach children's behavior and the world of emotions, as well as comparing traditional techniques used to manage behavior in schools to the more relational-based Emotion Coaching approach.

Chapter 3 goes on to clarify how to do Emotion Coaching. It explores in depth each of the four steps of Emotion Coaching identified by our research. As in all the chapters, its use is illustrated by a range of case studies taken from our research and from the ECUK practitioner trainers, which exemplify some of the intricacies and complexities of each of the steps.

Chapter 4 then looks at how adults can use Emotion Coaching more effectively by highlighting a number of different aspects which might affect how it can be applied to practice. This starts by exploring the concept of meta-emotion philosophy, which refers to adults' awareness of emotions, their awareness and acceptance of emotions in a child, and how they coach a child about the emotions. It also provides a number of helpful tips about when and how to use Emotion Coaching.

Chapter 5 introduces a practical framework which can help to plan and evaluate the use of Emotion Coaching in practice. It outlines the model of engagement and spectrum of use when working with children to adopt, adapt and sustain the use of Emotion Coaching practice.

The final chapter offers a range of supporting strategies that complement the use of Emotion Coaching. It references tried and tested strategies which, from research and practitioner feedback, have been used successfully alongside Emotion Coaching in practice.

This book is mostly written for practitioners but Emotion Coaching was originally conceived as a parenting style, and many of the practitioners who participated and contributed to this book are also parents or carers. Therefore, much of the content of this book is relevant to the use of Emotion Coaching in the home and we have occasionally drawn on examples from parents and carers. All names and some contextual details have been changed to protect the anonymity of the adults and children. Finally, for simplicity we have used the term 'children' to denote both children and young people.

....

Chapter 1

Why Do We Need Emotion Coaching?

Emotion Coaching is all about emotions and you can use it to help your everyday interactions with children and even adults. It can be a universal, supportive and empowering practice for working with other people's emotions, including challenging behaviors. In this chapter, we offer an explanation of why we have emotions and what they do; how emotions inform our thoughts and actions and how we learn to manage or regulate our emotions so that we can communicate more effectively with others.

We know that humans are social beings wanting, indeed needing, to communicate and socially engage with each other. Children's behavior reflects the ongoing interactions between experiences, environments and their relationships with adults—behaviors that change as we age. This chapter will suggest how relationships, experiences and environments influence our behavior and the way we communicate, and we'll make links to common behavioral patterns that we see in children.

Brain, body and behavior

We do not need to be brain scientists to do Emotion Coaching, but it really helps if we know a little about how our brains and bodies work together to create and respond to emotions. If we think about a typical brain, it undergoes relatively predictable developmental changes to structure and function, so why do we differ so much in our ability to regulate our emotions, our thoughts and our behavioral responses?

To begin to answer this question, and help us to better understand children's behavior, we need to have some understanding of the basic structures of the typical brain, how brains function and how, over time, they develop. There are two important systems that are involved in keeping us alive. There is the stress response system which drives survival through "protective" behavioral adjustments. And then there is the creative and "connective" social system, which supports survival through communicating and cooperation with others. These two systems work together to manage our emotional and behavioral responses which support survival and wellbeing.

In this chapter, we provide an explanation of how these two integrated systems are continuously influenced by our interpersonal relationships and environmental contexts. This perhaps offers some explanation as to why some people merely survive while others thrive. Emotion Coaching seems to work with, rather than against, our brains and bodies to help support emotional regulation and promote prosocial behaviors.

Brains or minds?

The words brain and mind are often used interchangeably, but it is useful to know the differences when we are looking at brains, emotions and behaviors.

The brain is a physical organ, weighing on average 1.5kg, and is made up of blood vessels and nerve cells. It is shaped like a walnut and, just like a walnut, it has two halves, known as right and left hemispheres. The brain, protected by the skull, coordinates movement, feelings and functions of the body (e.g. breathing, digestion, vision). It is where the information from the body, our environment and other people is constantly processed and used to keep us alive. As we grow older, there are typical, recognizable developmental changes to the brain's structure and function. Indeed, it is now believed that the brain is not fully mature until we are in our mid- to late twenties.

Our mind is intimately related to our brain but is invisible. It involves an individual's conscience, understanding and thought processes, and has tremendous power over all bodily systems. The mind reflects a combination of our brain's developmental stage, our experiences and engagement with the environment and other people as well as our interpretations of life's accumulated experiences and interactions. The mind both constructs (creates) and is constructed by our thoughts, feelings, memories and beliefs, all of which inform our behaviors.

Recent research suggests that there are interactive, reciprocal relationships between the brain (and so the mind), experiences, relationships and our environments (Porges, 2015; Siegel, 2012). By this we mean not only does the brain/mind influence our behavior responses to experiences, our environments and others, but these experiences, relationships and environments themselves can influence the subsequent development and construction of our brain. This suggests why it is so important to focus on promoting relationships, experiences and environments that nurture developing and learning brains, especially in childhood.

In the next section, the parts of a brain are described. Remember that as scientific advances are made, our knowledge and understanding about its structure and function keep changing.

What are learning brains?

When working with children, we want to understand "how they tick" to be able to provide them with relationships, experiences and environments that are both stimulating and rewarding. We know children learn from their relationships with others, and from their experiences and the environments in which they grow. They're influenced by their genetic inheritance as well. It is this combination and the quality of the relationships, experiences and environments that help build brains and minds. Therefore, having an understanding of how a typical brain grows and which relationships, experiences and environments affect development can help us to understand why Emotion Coaching is a useful strategy to support children's learning and behavior.

Put another way, think about when you take a car to a mechanic, whether for a routine service or because you're worried it is not performing as it should. You assume that the mechanic knows, at least, the basics of what makes an engine work—about the parts in an engine, how they work together and the performance expectations for different aged engines. You would also expect that the mechanic knows how to maintain an engine's performance, can identify common causes of poor performance and is able to offer advice to help you take care of the car.

When working with children, we too need to know how their learning "engines" (their brains) work. We need to have some awareness of the different parts of a brain, how they work together, what to expect from different ages of brains and how brain performance, and so the mind, typically develops over time. As adults, we need to be aware of common signs that suggest a child may need help and what practice or strategies will help to nurture optimal performance of the brain.

However, just as you do not expect the mechanic at the local garage to be a racing car specialist, you are not expected to be a brain specialist. But if you have a sufficient understanding of how brains typically function, this can inform your work and enable you to appreciate why strategies such as Emotion Coaching can help to support your practice and relationship with children.

Let's take a quick look at the different parts of a brain, the functions of a typical brain and what happens to our brains and minds as we grow and learn. Before we start, it is important to note that we're just highlighting some key aspects of the brain that can help us to understand children's emotions and behavior. Scientists are still developing our understanding of how the brain and body work together and we all need to be cautious about how we interpret current understanding.

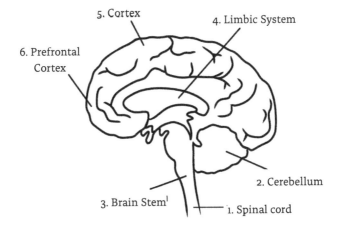

FIGURE 1.1 DIFFERENT PARTS OF THE BRAIN (© EMOTION COACHING UK)

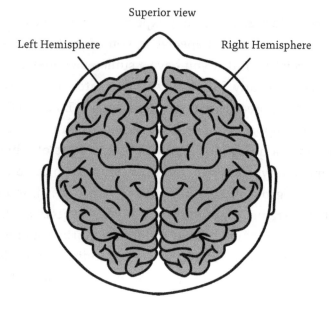

FIGURE 1.2 TWO HEMISPHERES OF THE BRAIN
(© EMOTION COACHING UK)

Although individual brains do differ slightly, the typical brain has a recognizable structure, shown in Figures 1.1 and 1.2. The brain is made up of two halves or hemispheres. Each of these hemispheres is split into four lobes and each lobe may be split again into areas of specialized but not exclusive function. Although the lobes do have recognizable, dedicated functions, it is now believed that they are not exclusive and work together. The two hemispheres also work together, connected by the corpus callosum, which acts like a bridge, allowing information to pass easily between the two hemispheres. The importance of this connection will be explained later in the chapter.

Let's now take a closer look at the different brain regions (numbered 1–6 on Figure 1.1) to see what they do.

1. Spinal cord: This contains nerves carrying sensory information to be processed by the brain, constantly, from all parts of the body. The brain translates all the information, deciding what response is to be taken, and sends information back down to inform actions and behavior.

2. Cerebellum: This receives information from the sensory systems, coordinating movements and integrating bodily information with emotional and cognitive processing. This includes eye movements, speech, posture, balance and coordination.

3. Brain stem: This area receives information from the body and relays it to the rest of the brain. It is responsible for unconscious activities that regulate and keep us alive, for example levels of brain alertness, breathing, heart rate and blood pressure. It also facilitates our fight/flight/freeze stress or survival response.

4. Limbic system: This area lies deep inside the brain. It is an area that is important in motivation, behavioral regulation and activating our stress response (our fight/flight/freeze survival response). The amygdala is the part of the limbic region which focuses on giving sensory information an emotional "label," so helping to identify and speed up our thinking and responses. Most importantly, to support survival our brains are hardwired to recognize and respond to the emotions of distress, fear, anger, surprise, disgust and joy (Ekman, 2016)—this means they cannot be ignored. When there is a physical or psychological threat or danger, the amygdala alerts the hypothalamus, another important region of the brain, to automatically release chemicals (hormones) to prepare and support survival behaviors. The hippocampus is another part in the limbic region and is involved in creating and maintaining memories. It seems to play a role in emotional appraisal by referencing previous experiences to help guide and inform future decisions and actions.

5. Cortex: This is the area of the brain that we see when we look at the surface of a whole brain. It is the outside layer and appears greyish and wrinkled with infolds on the surface. Known also as the "thinking brain," this is responsible for our perceiving, understanding, reasoning, processing and responding to all sensory information, including speech and language.

6. Prefrontal cortex: This is an area of the cortex that is at the front of the brain (so just behind the forehead). It is particularly responsible for complex cognitive behaviors such as problem-solving, rationality, decision-making, attention span, judgement, personality expression and our ability to moderate social behaviors. This part of the brain is the last to fully establish function and it is not until our mid-twenties that this area is considered fully mature. It is important to note that the cortex and prefrontal cortex are well connected to the limbic system and all these regions are integrated in learning, decision-making and behaviors.

Now we know the main areas of the brain and their functions, we need a way to remember how they are connected and work with one another.

To help visualize the brain (as in Figure 1.1) and to see how the different parts can work together, Dan Siegel (2012) created a simple model using a hand! So, let's get physical and roll up our sleeves to reveal a hand model of the brain to share with others—including the children you work with.

The hand model of the brain

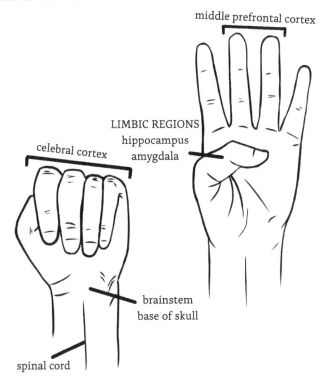

FIGURE 1.3 THE HAND MODEL OF THE BRAIN (© EMOTION COACHING UK)

Figure 1.3 shows you a simple way to visualize the important parts of the brain and how they are connected and work together. (The numbers in the description below refer back to the parts of the brain shown in Figure 1.1.)

First, place your elbow on a hard surface so your forearm is pointing upwards. Have your hand with the palm facing you, your hand out flat with the tips of your fingers pointing upwards.

The arm and wrist represent your spinal cord (1). As noted earlier, the spinal cord relays, consciously and unconsciously, messages and sensations to and from the body and brain. The palm of the hand is the cerebellum (2) and brainstem (3). These parts of the brain control many of the unconscious functions of the body (such as breathing, blood pressure, posture and blood flow). The brainstem is also involved in supporting the innate stress response system (to promote fight/flight/freeze behaviors).

Now fold your thumb in, so it is tucked into the palm of your hand; feel how close and connected it is to the palm of your hand.
The thumb represents your limbic system (4). All sensory information received is given an emotional label, to help speed up and guide the brain to appropriately respond.

Siegel and Payne Bryson (2012) call the cerebellum, brainstem and limbic system (so your palm and thumb) the "downstairs" brain. It is also sometimes referred to as the "emotional brain" because it is intimately involved in generating and controlling emotional responses. These parts are tucked away below our "upstairs" or "thinking brain," which we will now explore.

Now curl your fingers over and around your thumb, notice how your fingers touch and connect with your thumb and brush the palm of your hand.
The back of your hand and your fingers represent the cortex (5) and the fingertips are the prefrontal cortex (6). Remember, the cortex, and especially the prefrontal cortex, is considered to be the "reasoning or thinking brain," involved in cognition. This is a functionally complex part of the brain, allowing us to consciously control behaviors, thoughts and actions. Crucially, the prefrontal lobes help to regulate our emotional responses; allow us to understand, cooperate and socially engage with others; and this is our preferred way to communicate, problem-solve and learn. The ability to understand the intention of others and the desire to socially engage is considered a unique and necessary skill in humans. Siegel and Payne Bryson (2012) call this part of the brain (cortex and prefrontal cortex) the "upstairs" brain.

As we recognize that different areas of the brain may have

differing functions, you may wonder how and why they work together. Perhaps you know the saying "the whole is greater than the sum of the parts"? Well, the brain is most efficient when its parts are working together effectively to inform thinking, decision-making, actions and behaviors.

How the hand model of the brain can help explain our behavior

We prefer to share experiences and problem-solve with others through social engagement. When you feel sufficiently safe and secure in your environment and relationships, energies can be focused on the task or learning in hand. When the emotional and rational parts of the brain work together to access memories and experiences effectively, we are more willing and able to try new experiences and challenges, and be ready to learn.

Looking at the hand model, when we make that fist with our thumb tucked under our fingers (Figure 1.3) we can feel that the parts of the brain are connected to look like an intact brain.

In this state, the brain can be regarded as a "learning brain" because the parts of the brain are connected and can work effectively. As we grow older, the connections between the different parts of the brain become stronger and more established. However, our relationships, experiences and environments will influence the development and strength of these connections.

The brain is integral to learning but its primary role is to keep us safe—to support our survival. But how does it do this? We are continuously and largely unconsciously (so we are not usually aware of it happening) checking our environment and watching those around us to identify anyone or anything that might be a threat to our existence. If the brain senses a threat (a stressor) that cannot be resolved through using social and communication skills (so using our social engagement system), it moves into a state of high alert or alarm. This activates the stress response system (also known as the fight/flight/freeze response) to prioritize and support protective thinking and behavior. It's important to note that a threat can be both real and perceived—someone being rude to you is not a major threat to survival, but you may feel affronted and your sense of self threatened. What you do about it will depend on how you regulate your emotional response or behavior—you may not go into full fight/flight/freeze but use your social engagement system to manage and resolve the issue. Or you may find that you respond through activating your stress response system and try to resolve the situation through attack or by moving away.

What's happening in the brain and body when the stress response system is activated?

Flip the fingers away from your thumb, so they are pointing upwards; this represents what happens to the brain in response to activation of the stress response system.

As you can see, the connections between the thinking brain (prefrontal cortex, 6) and emotional (limbic, 4) system are no longer so close, and the survival instinct part of the brain (the limbic system and the cerebellum, 3) now takes control of our behavioral response. It becomes more difficult to make the considered, sensible and prosocial decisions made when the limbic system and the prefrontal cortex are connected and working together. Without this close interaction, decisions become more impulsive and appear less rational.

In response to a state of danger or alarm, hormones are automatically released into the bloodstream to prepare the body to take immediate action. This results in an increase in blood pressure, heartbeat and blood flow to the limbs, and there is an increased breakdown of protein along with a mobilization of fats and sugars into the bloodstream to increase energy levels. Our sensitivity to and focus on our environment and others who may be potential threats increases. Behavior is focused on survival through mobilizing actions to attack (fight) or to run away from the stressor (flight). However, if the brain believes that neither fight nor flight will support survival, the least effective defense mechanism is for the body to shut down (freeze). This can lead to unresponsiveness and a loss of function or mobility. Remember that the stress response system operates on a kind of spectrum—we don't always go into full flight/fight mode, although some of us might.

When the stress response system is activated, our bodies can physically "tune out" of listening to human voice frequency and "tune in" to other sounds, to help locate and focus on the immediate danger. Attention narrows to concentrate on the potential dangers in the immediate surroundings and in other people. Look again at what happens when you flip your fingers upwards; you may have used or heard the phrase when someone's behavior appears unpredictable and irrational, "Wow, they've flipped their lid." In part, this is exactly what has happened as their behaviors and actions are largely driven by the innate but restrictive survival responses, rather than involving rational and creative thought and problem solving. But again, remember that not everyone will necessarily completely "flip their lid" and it doesn't mean that there is a complete disconnection between the "upstairs" (thinking) and "downstairs" (feelings and stress response) parts of the brain.

Now, curl your fingers back around the thumb (limbic system), and see how the parts of the brain reconnect. The brain has returned to its preferred learning state.

The stress response system is designed for survival emergencies only and uses lots of energy to function effectively. Consequently, when it is activated, other brain and body functions are temporarily compromised in order to conserve energy. Once the threat is over, the vagus nerve acts as the counterpart to our stress response system.

The vagus nerve originates in the brain and branches out in multiple directions to the face, neck and into most organs of the body. It continuously carries messages and information to and from the organs and brain, influencing our hearing, speech, swallowing, digestion and immune response. When we are not under stress or threat, the vagus nerve is the primary control that allows the body to rest, relax and socially engage. Also, once a threat/danger is over and having established that the environment and relationships are safe, it triggers responses to help the body and brain to emotionally and physically calm down. This returns bodily and brain systems back to their normal function, and attention can return to social and environmental engagement. We will discuss the vagus nerve's important role in regulating emotional responses in a later section, "Building brains."

The brain connections, particularly between the prefrontal cortex and the limbic system, permit two-way communication, helping to dampen-down or manage our stress response system while continuing to be able to respond quickly to danger and threat. For example, these connections allow us to respond appropriately and then calm down and allow our ears to re-tune to human voice frequency. We all need quick, appropriate and effective responses to genuine threats (e.g. someone about to hit us) but we also need to develop quick, appropriate and effective responses to perceived threats (e.g. imagining monsters under our bed). In both cases, we need to be able to calm down and return to the learning brain state to show socially appropriate behavior.

A child in a tantrum or a child refusing to line up in the classroom has "flipped their lid" in some way and needs calming down and supporting to manage and improve their behavioral response. The brain hand model helps us to visualize the different parts of the brain, how they are connected and how the brain and body can work together to support positive behaviors. Children seem to relate well to the visual representation of the model, and it can be used as an empowering tool to support calming and improve behavioral responses.

Amanda, a teacher of four- and five-year-old children was exploring the links between the brain, body and emotions as part of the term's focus on mental health and wellbeing. As part of this, she and the teaching assistant regularly used Emotion Coaching with the pupils, individually and as a class. The brain hand model supported conversations throughout the school day about how the children felt and helped to explain what was going on in their bodies and brains. After a month, Amanda observed two of her pupils coming in from play. Jess was talking to Anna; he was flipping his fingers up and down and saying, "I think you're angry because she pushed you and took the ball. I bet you're feeling like this (fingers pointing straight up). Miss understands—she told us it can happen to all of us (flipping his fingers up and down). If you go to Miss she'll know and she'll make you feel better, like this (he tucked in his thumb and curled his fingers to make a fist)."

Can we learn to recognize and respond appropriately to threat? Yes. As mentioned earlier, we are born with an innate and immediate response to stressors; however, we are also born expecting our carers to "look out for us" and protect us until we can protect ourselves. Therefore, we learn when to respond, how to respond and what to do in response to stressors from "significant others" in our lives. Our brain's ability to do so develops over time, through experience and in response to our relationships and the environments we live in. Therefore, as practitioners, we do need to understand a little about how brains operate to support learning, and in turn, how learning supports brain development.

How do brains work?

Neurones and neuronal networks

Let's now look at what we know about how the brain supports learning. Our central nervous system is made up of the spinal cord and the brain and information is relayed to and from our brains, our bodies and our senses. Our brain makes sense of what is happening around and inside us, and then organizes and stores this information for future use. These processes mean we can access, assess and take appropriate actions to respond to the situations we find ourselves in.

In early childhood, we learn how to respond and organize our behaviors through observation and copying others, and through engagement and repetition of experiences and environments. As children grow older, the brain physically matures, becoming functionally more complex and creative, allowing reason to construct ideas and thoughts to inform decisions and behaviors. Indeed, childhood is the time when brains grow and change most rapidly. It is the time when the brain is most receptive, responsive and influenced by environments, experiences and relationships. It can be said that in childhood, and indeed throughout our lives, we live to learn and in doing so, are learning how to live (Gilbert *et al.*, 2013).

As discussed earlier, the different areas of the brain are connected. This allows information about our experiences, relationships and environments, including our internal body environment as well as the environments we live in, to be assessed, stored and shared to inform our decisions and behaviors. Connections are created via "neurones," which are cells that allow information to pass along themselves as electrical impulses. Neurones carry information throughout the human body, from the senses to the central nervous system, from one place in the central nervous system to another and from the central nervous system to the muscles.

Neurones carry information and when sufficiently stimulated ("fired") are able to transmit the information to other neurones, so neurones can communicate with one another. This connecting and communication of neurones creates neuronal networks which allow information to be shared across the central nervous system. Neuronal networks build children's mental representation of the world, people and relationships, which informs their decision-making, actions and behaviors.

Collectively, neuronal networks in the brain are known as the connectome. You can imagine the connectome as a road transport network, joining up towns and cities. How quickly you can travel along roads depends on their size and their connections to other roads. Usually, the bigger the road, the more roads can connect to it and the easier and quicker it is to travel from one place to another. Routes that are frequently traveled become the preferred routes and in doing so become more familiar, easier to navigate and so even quicker to travel along. Neuronal networks are like the road transport system for the brain, and strong, well-connected neuronal networks are easier to access and quicker for information to travel along. Repeated use leads to these networks becoming the preferred routes, which are more sensitive and need less stimulation to become activated. Over time, this leads to thoughts, actions and behaviors happening quicker and becoming more automated as a response. It needs to be remembered that neuronal networks will adapt to create appropriate behavioral responses to support survival in the environment, experiences and relationships we find ourselves in—whether they are nurturing or detrimental.

Tuning and pruning neuronal networks

From birth, much energy is given to developing strong neuronal networks to connect the areas of the brain. Children are born with many neurones and neuronal networks, but they have restricted connectivity. Repeated stimulation from experiences, environments and relationships develops connectivity and improves their responsiveness and efficiency in carrying information. Well-connected and frequently used networks need less stimulation to become activated, so information can be transmitted faster and with less effort. In this way, certain thinking and behaviors become effortless and automatic responses.

However, our bodies need to use energy efficiently, and building and maintaining neuronal networks requires a lot of energy. If neuronal networks are not regularly stimulated by use, the neurones and networks do not develop strong connections, so information travels along them more slowly. Just imagine a road that is narrow, with few junctions to connect to other roads. You are less likely to choose this road for travel if there is an alternative that is faster because it is wider and has lots of junctions.

If neuronal networks are not activated or are under-used over a long period of time, a natural brain process called pruning occurs. This minimizes wastage of resources and, although essential for effective use of available energy, it is an indiscriminate process. It does not differentiate neurons and neuronal networks that are needed for the child's potential development. Fewer neurons mean less opportunity to process information, so compromising connectivity and learning potential. As the old adage goes—use it or lose it.

Plasticity and mirroring

Neuronal networks in the brain are continually adapting and changing in response to ongoing environments, experiences and relationships. The brain's ability to grow, adapt and change its structural connections and sensitivity to information stimulation is known as plasticity. Brain plasticity is greatest in childhood; however, it continues, albeit more slowly, throughout life.

Plasticity allows the brain to learn, and keep learning, from all our experiences, environments and engaging with others to ensure survival. Although brain functionality is determined in part by genetics, it also develops through maturation. Furthermore, there is a developmental expectation that the brain will be stimulated through trial and error and repeated exposures and experiences. Just because a child appears to have a repeated fixed response to particular situations, it does not mean this will remain the only way they can respond. Through repeated, alternative interactions and differing experiences with others, new neuronal pathways can be established to support new behavioral responses. Therefore, the quality of relationships, the opportunities for experiences and type of environments will all influence the quality and capacity of a child's learning.

There is an expectation, particularly in children, that significant adults in our lives will care for us, so that we can learn how to care for ourselves and eventually others. Mirroring is our natural ability to learn through watching and copying others. To mimic, we need skills to be able to recognize and interpret the actions and intentions of those around. Therefore, as humans, we must have brain mechanisms involving neuronal networks that support our understanding of the motor actions of others and also help us to interpret their intentions. Think about how we learn to smile—repeatedly watching others smile at them eventually builds a mirroring response in a child. Through experience, babies start to learn about the intention behind that smile and, by contextualizing, use it to inform their own responses and it becomes part of their social engagement system. We don't formally teach a baby to smile—it just happens over time through their relationships, environment and experiences.

How exactly we understand actions and interpret the intentions of others is complex and remains a subject of scientific debate, but, for the purposes of this book, it has important implications for how we act as role models for children. Emotion Coaching can be a powerful way of modeling socially appropriate behaviors. Thinking back to Jess and Anna. Jess had both experienced and watched how the adults in his classroom responded to children's emotional moments. Every time he noticed this happening, his mirroring system was activated, and frequent activation meant that a pattern of neuronal connections in his brain strengthened. Jess was able to remember what he had seen and experienced and respond to Anna in a similar way by mimicking his role models. Another example comes from a four-year-old who started to use Emotion Coaching when playing with dolls in the home corner as a result of adults modeling Emotion Coaching in a nursery setting. The adult recalls the child saying, "You're really upset because your ribbon fell off your head. I've had that before. I'll give you a cuddle and kiss."

We'll revisit this point when we talk about the importance of modeling empathy later in the book, but it's worth noting here that in order to respond and communicate effectively, and get our personal and societal needs met, we need skills to be able to recognize and understand what others around us are feeling and thinking. We need to develop empathy, which essentially involves a personal capacity to think, understand and share in the emotions and feelings of others.

Empathy is an ability to put ourselves "in someone else's shoes." Understanding the intentions, thoughts and feelings of others that are informing their behaviors is essential in supporting effective socialization and the development of prosocial relationships. However, unlike the basic emotions that are hardwired at birth, we need to experience empathy to be able to show empathy.

It is through our experiences, environments and relationships that we develop our skills to understand and engage with others. Emotion Coaching supports the development of empathy in children by adults modeling empathic responses around them.

Building brains

It needs to be remembered that brain development is complex and not fully understood, with many processes operating simultaneously over periods of time. We mentioned earlier that the brain is wired to learn, and childhood is a period when the brain has its greatest plasticity and capacity to learn. Brain functionality typically develops as we grow older, but this is dependant on the expectation that the brain will be stimulated through trial and error and repeated exposures and experiences. Therefore, as the next section shows, the quality of relationships, the opportunities for experiences and type of environments all influence what children learn and their learning capacity.

The vagus nerve and vagal tone

Children's ongoing health and wellbeing reflects integration and interaction between their social engagement system and stress response system. The sympathetic nervous system controls our stress response system (fight/flight behaviors), which is automatically activated when we feel unsafe or sense real or perceived danger. The parasympathetic nervous system, primarily through the vagus nerve, controls our social engagement system (including rational thought and learning) as well as acting as a counterbalance to our stress response system.

When we feel safe, and not stressed, the vagus nerve is in control, sending commands to our internal organs to rest easy and to allow recuperation. In this state, we can use our brain and energies to engage and communicate with others and our surroundings, to think creatively, to concentrate and to learn.

A child's ability to regulate their stress response so as to be able to engage appropriately within the social world is known as vagal tone (Gottman *et al.*, 1997; Porges, 2011). Vagal tone is, in part, genetic, but also reflects brain maturation and the environmental, experiential and relational experiences of the child. As we have mentioned earlier, we know that different areas of the brain mature at different rates. A child's prefrontal lobes (upstairs brain), involved in reasoning, thinking, understanding and managing our social engagement system, are functionally less mature at birth than their limbic system (downstairs brain), which controls the stress response system. Therefore, children are easily overwhelmed with new and challenging experiences. Emotional responses, driven primarily by their limbic system (downstairs brain) quickly lead to physical distress as they struggle to feel calm. To effectively manage emotions, children need time and opportunity to develop robust neuronal network connections between their prefrontal lobes (thinking brain) and the limbic system (emotional brain)— they need good vagal tone.

Children with effective, responsive vagal tone have better emotional balance (they are able to assess and respond appropriately), clearer thinking, improved attention, a more efficient immune system (as energy is available to maintain it rather than support the stress response) and greater resilience in the face of adversity (Gottman *et al.*, 1997). To develop integrated and effective social engagement and stress response systems, in other words good vagal tone, children need time, opportunities and support to develop and learn to connect, interact and understand others, to make sense of social relationships and enjoy social relationships. They need to learn to assess and respond appropriately (behavior) and be shown how to regulate their emotional responses (stressors).

Although there is an inherited element to vagal tone, its development is also supported through children experiencing early relationships and attachments that offer consistent, soothing, compassion and physical comfort—in other words nurturing. When distressed, adult co-regulation helps to trigger the child's vagus nerve, assisting them to physically and emotionally calm down.

Co-regulation involves being present and responsive to a child's needs in the moment of stress. It is through this interpersonal process that the adult organizes the stressful moments, helping the child to live through and manage experiences that at first appear novel and alarming.

Think about how we comfort a crying baby and solve the cause of their distress. As a child matures and through repeated and consistent co-regulation, they learn to self-soothe and eventually self-regulate. Shanker (2016) describes self-regulation as the ability to manage stress levels, emotions, behavior and attention so that we're able to achieve goals and engage in learning, behave in socially acceptable ways and maintain good relationships. Self-regulatory skills therefore help children to manage their emotions, behaviors and thoughts, particularly disruptive and impulsive ones, despite the challenges and unpredictability of the world around them. They enable children to participate and effectively engage with others and have conscious control of their thoughts, feelings and behavior.

Co-regulation is usually provided by a child's parents and carers, but other significant adults in a child's life, such as practitioners and other close adults, can help to activate and develop a child's vagal tone. This is discussed further in the next chapter.

Relationships matter

As we have said, children need time with sufficiently consistent, caring and trusting adults to guide them and to help them to calm down. This in turn helps them to learn to self-soothe. These types of relationships are known as attuned relationships, where the child's emotional and bodily states are the focus of the adult's empathic attention.

Empathic adults teach a child, through their actions and deeds, how to be aware of their feelings, how to assess the stressors in their lives, how to calm and manage the stressors, and how to respond appropriately. In other words, empathic adults work with the child's social engagement and stress response system to help them learn self-regulation. When an adult is attuned to a child's distressed emotional and bodily states, their empathic response helps the child to feel seen and soothed. This promotes a sense of "felt" safety and security, triggering their vagus nerve, so helping the child to start to calm. As a child grows, consistent and repeated empathic, attuned and nurturing relationships enable them to understand their own and others' emotions better. Through being co-regulated when distressed, they learn and practice emotional regulation and develop strategies (neuronal networks in the brain) to manage emotional distress, by calming their stress response system and activating their social engagement system.

Challenging childhood experiences

Adapting our behavior to ensure survival is what we do all the time. This means that we are all constantly checking our surroundings and looking to others for cues about whether we are safe or not. This happens largely unconsciously (we are not aware we are doing it) and is known as neuroception (Porges, 2011). To help our brain distinguish safety and danger, we look at others' movements, voice tone, facial expressions, head and hand movements, touch, as well as our own feelings—our internal body states.

For survival, children have to learn to accurately match what they see and feel with actual risk. When we feel safe, the stress response system, limited to fight and flight behavioral responses, is inhibited. The social engagement system, our preferred behavioral system, dominates (think back to the hand model of the brain—the learning brain is when the brain is modeled as a fist and all parts are communicating and working together). In this state, the health and function of the brain, body and mind are optimized, and complex activities such as planning, decision-making, problem-solving and self-control can be accessed to inform our behaviors.

Through our own responses, adults can help children to learn and assess danger and learn using their own social engagement system rather than immediately activating their stress response system. Here is an example:

Tracey was out in the garden with Priti and Dom on a November afternoon. They were collecting leaves for painting when all of a sudden there was a loud "bang" from next door's garden. Priti and Dom immediately stopped picking up leaves and quickly looked up at Tracey. Tracey turned to them, bent down and said to them both, in a soft, calm voice, "Ah, that was a loud and unexpected noise just then, we weren't expecting that, but it's okay, we're safe. It's probably just some people getting excited and practicing for Guy Fawkes night, which is coming up in a few days. You know, Guy Fawkes day is celebrated with lots of fireworks which make loud noises and when it's dark you can see all their pretty colours." Priti and Dom nodded and returned to looking for leaves.

However, if Tracey had responded by looking alarmed and screaming, these actions would have confirmed Priti and Dom's neuroception alarm that they were indeed in real danger, and their stress response system (fight/flight behaviors) would have automatically been activated and dominated their behavior.

What needs to be remembered is that the brain prioritises learning that optimizes survival, and does not discriminate between nurturing and detrimental learning experiences. Therefore, if a child does not have opportunities in their relationships and environments to feel and be seen, safe, soothed or secure (Siegel and Payne Bryson

2012), and regularly feels alone, unsafe, dysregulated or insecure, their learning may become driven by the stress response system.

Children who experience multiple or consistent adverse experiences and hostile environments, commonly known as adverse childhood experiences, without sufficient empathic adults or attuned relationships, prioritize learning behavioral and thought repertoires to support survival in their world. They have fewer opportunities to learn and practice assessing safety and regulating their emotional response to connect, trust, relax and engage socially. They have fewer opportunities to develop and strengthen the connections between the limbic system, which controls the stress response system and the rational, reasoning prefrontal lobes which regulate our social engagement system. These children come to rely on behaviors and actions driven by the more impulsive and less rational limbic system.

Frequent activation of their stress response system means neuronal networks become wired to be sensitive to stressors and vigilant to potential danger. They learn to be constantly on "high alert" and may respond more quickly than others to activate emotional and behavioral responses for survival (fight/flight actions) which may not be socially appropriate or effective.

Without access to and experience of the "tools" to effectively engage and support social engagement, children find managing relationships with others difficult and subsequent educational experience potentially stressful. Indeed, with severe, prolonged trauma there is a primitive survival response that can be activated. This is known as the "freeze response" and unlike the fight/flight response, which is all about taking action and mobility, this response leads to survival through immobility and extreme disengagement from relationships and environments.

Emotion Coaching seems to work with the body and brain by acting as a vehicle for co-regulating emotional distress, supporting the child to feel calm and to re-engage in social interactions. In a calm state, children are better able to make sense of what they feel, how they and others respond and problem-solve. Consistent and empathic responses, such as Emotion Coaching by adults in emotional moments, help build effective toolkits for life for all children.

Connections, contributions, co-construction and creativity

This chapter offers a simplified explanation of how children's brains and minds develop and function. It contains a lot of information and is designed to be revisited many times on your Emotion Coaching journey.

To help remember the key qualities and functions of the brains think of the four Cs:

1. Connections: The connections between neurones and neuronal networks need to be established, extensive and efficient to utilize the whole of the brain's capacity.

2. Contributions: Children live and learn from relationships with empathic and attuned significant others to manage their social engagement and stress response systems. Through role models, copying, trial and error and cooperation, developing brains are strengthened and shaped.

3. Co-construction: The functional efficiency of brains reflects the co-construction between genes, environments, experiences and relationships. Through co-regulation comes self-regulation, which is an evolving, ongoing, lifelong process.

4. Creativity: To promote brain health and wellbeing, children need to feel seen, safe, soothed and secure (Siegel and Payne

Bryson, 2012). They can then personally engage in learning environments, experiences and relationships that are nurturing, multi-sensory, rewarding, motivating, interesting and fun.

(Adapted from Rose, Gilbert and Richards, 2015)

Chapter 2

What Is Emotion Coaching?

Now that we have looked at why Emotion Coaching can help us with our work with children, we need to look more closely at what it is. This chapter traces the origins of Emotion Coaching as a parenting style, outlining how we translated the work of Gottman and his colleagues (1996, 1997) into educational settings and developed a four-stepped framework for this approach. The chapter illustrates how effective Emotion Coaching and a relational approach to managing behaviour can be in supporting children's resilience and wellbeing.

A simple definition

Put simply, Emotion Coaching is a way of communicating with a child who is struggling to manage their emotions. Their distress may be shown in a variety of ways—they might seem withdrawn and distracted, behaving rudely or disruptive and unable to join in. John Gottman explains that Emotion Coaching is about helping children to understand the different emotions they experience, why they occur, and how to handle them (Gottman and DeClaire, 1997).

Emotion Coaching is particularly concerned with helping

children to regulate how they feel, which can then help them regulate how they behave. It focuses attention on the feelings which are driving the behavior, not just the behavior itself.

Where did Emotion Coaching come from?

A key message about Emotion Coaching is that it was not created—it was observed. In other words, it is a naturally occurring way for people to communicate with others during times of distress. John Gottman and his colleagues (Gottman *et al.*, 1997) coined the phrase "Emotion Coaching" to describe the manner in which some parents naturally engaged with their children. They were looking, in particular, not at how parents responded to children's behavior—as most parenting research has done—but how parents engaged with their children's emotions.

They noticed that particular parents responded differently to their children's emotions. They observed that some parents' (who they labeled Emotion Coaching parents) responses seemed to give their children advantage in a variety of ways. The research showed that children of Emotion Coaching parents:

- achieve more academically in school

- are more popular

- have fewer behavioral problems

- have fewer infectious illnesses

- are more emotionally stable

- are more resilient.

Children who experience Emotion Coaching are more able, for example, to control their impulses, to self soothe when they get upset, and to delay gratification. These skills help to regulate how they feel and how they behave, which enables them in turn to focus their attention, concentrate and resist distractions. You can see why Emotion Coached children have more friends and do better in school. Interestingly, they also appear to have better health, which may be because they are able to regulate their stress response more easily. In all, Emotion Coached children appear to be able to cope more effectively with life's ups and downs.

If Emotion Coaching is a parenting style, why do it in school?

When we discovered Emotion Coaching, we realized it could also be a very useful strategy to help children in schools, early years settings and youth centers. So, through research, we started to try to understand its impact on a range of school and early years practitioners, as well as professionals working in the community, such as social workers and health visitors. Our studies found that when adults used Emotion Coaching it had a positive impact on both children and adults (Gilbert, 2018; Rose, Gilbert and McGuire-Snieckus, 2015; Gus, 2018a). Specifically, we found that Emotion Coaching:

- helps children to regulate, improve and take ownership of their behavior

- helps children to calm down and better understand their emotions

- helps practitioners to be more sensitive to children's needs

- helps create more consistent responses to children's behavior

- helps practitioners to feel more "in control" during incidents

- helps promote positive relationships between adults and children through promoting trust

- accelerated academic achievement.

For example, one practitioner talked about how Emotion Coaching helped her to communicate more effectively and consistently with children in stressful situations and to de-escalate volatile situations. She said, "It made the whole situation feel less fraught for both parties." By using Emotion Coaching, adults found managing difficult emotional situations less stressful and exhausting, with a positive impact not just on the children's wellbeing, but on their own. Another practitioner said, "It actually made me feel better because it made me feel calmer during the process." Yet another found that, "I show more empathy with how the child must be feeling and it helps you slow down to consider why a child is upset or angry. Because I now use this, I think the relationship I have with the children is much more relaxed."

What does Emotion Coaching involve?

For Gottman and his colleagues (1997), Emotion Coaching essentially involved five elements:

1. Be aware of a child's responses. This is about noticing, not just the behavior they might be displaying, but also their feelings. It's about tuning into the child in the moment they are feeling distress.

2. Recognize emotional times as opportunities for intimacy and teaching. Emotion Coaching uses times of distress as a chance to relate to the child in a positive way as well as a time to teach them about their feelings and behavior.

3. Listen empathically and validate the child's feelings. This is a critical part of Emotion Coaching. It's about the way in which the adult listens to the child, empathizes with them and validates how they might be feeling.

4. Help the child to verbally label their emotions. This may simply involve naming the emotion the child might be feeling or could be more exploratory by being suggestive about the feeling or helping the child to identify what they are feeling. Research has shown that naming emotions can be a powerful way to develop emotional literacy and become a tool to help regulate difficult feelings (Siegel and Payne Bryson, 2012).

5. Set limits while helping the child to problem-solve. It is important to note that Emotion Coaching is not just about engaging with how children are feeling, it also includes learning about school rules and setting boundaries around their behaviors. However, Emotion Coaching doesn't just set limits, it also involves problem-solving with the child to find different ways to manage their feelings. In this way, the child learns that strong emotions are normal, and that they can be managed by learning the skills to do so.

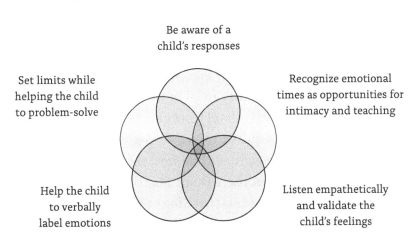

FIGURE 2.1 ELEMENTS OF EMOTION COACHING

In our research, we found that practitioners wanted more emphasis on the limit-setting and problem-solving elements of Emotion Coaching, so we initially proposed a three-step approach but revised this to become a four-step approach (Gus and Woods, 2017, Rose, Gilbert and McGuire-Snieckus, 2015).

Steps of Emotion Coaching:

1. Recognizing the child's feelings and empathizing with them.

2. Validating and label the feelings.

3. Setting limits on behavior (if needed).

4. Problem-solving with the child.

These four steps are explored in more detail in the next chapter, but it is important that they are not interpreted too restrictively. Emotion Coaching is not a rigid, step-by-step approach. It is a way of communicating in an empathic way to support a child and help them to manage their own feelings and behavior. It is also very adaptable to different situations. For example, you might find that you need only to utilize the first two steps in a situation with a child who is feeling worried about something. Talking about how they are feeling with someone who cares might be all they need for reassurance and to soothe their emotional stress. Older children, in particular, may not feel they need or want Steps 3 and 4—they probably already know the school rules and don't need reminding. Teenagers often prefer adults to show empathy and acknowledge their feelings and, once calmer, then find their own solutions to the problem that has upset them (Katz, Maliken and Stettler, 2012).

Another key point to note is that Steps 3 and 4 don't necessarily need to be undertaken in a strict order or completed immediately. Sometimes, Step 3 has to take precedence, for example if a child's safety is at risk. We may have to intervene during particularly volatile incidents and initially halt the behavior, before moving on to Step 1 and 2 to help the child to calm.

More of the practicalities of doing Emotion Coaching with children are considered in the next chapter but one final point to note at this stage is that sometimes the steps may be spread out over time. You might, for example, undertake Step 4 at a later time with an older child, reflecting back on the incident together and figuring out other solutions.

Empathizing with the feeling, not the behavior

A common concern regarding the practice of Emotion Coaching is the fear that empathizing during instances of "misbehavior" might give the appearance of endorsing the negative behavior. We are often asked, "Will all that empathizing just mean children will think it's okay to behave badly?" However, it's important to remember that Emotion Coaching is about empathizing with, acknowledging and validating the feeling, not the behavior. Remember also that Emotion Coaching is about setting limits on inappropriate behavior and problem-solving to provide alternative ways of behaving. So, you can acknowledge the feeling underlying the behavior, but not the behavior itself.

Another concern is that adults might feel "weak" and less in control if they empathize with a child who is misbehaving. They worry that if they are not stern and show disapproval then a child will not realize what they're doing is wrong. But again, it is important to recognize that Emotion Coaching includes setting boundaries, making it clear what is acceptable and appropriate behavior, as well as helping the child to behave differently next time they "flip their lid."

One of the most well-remembered quotes we had from a practitioner during our research was that she felt "more in control, but less controlling." When we asked the practitioner to elaborate, she explained that Emotion Coaching allowed her to manage situations and to maintain her authority, without having to assert her power, but still to feel that she had control. Previously she had needed to show a child "who was boss" and that "a child had to learn they can't get away with it." However, she now realized that promoting a learning environment was not about being more powerful than the children. It was about feeling in control of her own emotions and behavior so that she could help and guide the child to manage their own. She also commented that you need to be "stronger to be an emotion coach" as it was "very easy to just give in to my anger as I just wanted the behavior to stop."

We'll explore more about how Emotion Coaching affects adults' ability to regulate their own feelings and helps them to feel more able to manage challenging behavior in Chapter 5.

Empathy and guidance

Emotion Coaching views all behavior as a form of communication and makes an important distinction between children's behavior and the feelings that underlie that behavior. A key belief is that all emotions are acceptable, but not all consequent behaviors are appropriate. Emotion Coaching is essentially driven by two key elements: empathy and guidance, and these two elements underpin the adults' approach.

Emotion Coaching is an "in the moment" strategy to help manage and calm children's difficult emotions as well as an approach to support the development of emotional self-regulation. Empathy involves recognizing, labeling and validating a child's emotions, regardless of the behavior, in order to encourage self-awareness of their emotions. Adults who are "mind-minded"—that is, who tune into young children's thoughts and feelings—can help to scaffold children's understanding of their feelings and behavior.

As we have already noted, the circumstances could also require guidance on acceptable behavior and setting limits. This may involve stating clearly what is appropriate behavior. It might even lead to a consequential action such as some kind of sanction, although this would very much depend on the context and child and we wouldn't advocate simple use of sanctions for children who have experienced trauma. Emotion Coaching involves positive guidance rather than control. Engagement with the child in problem-solving (when they are responsive to it) supports their ability to learn to self-regulate and to seek other courses of action to promote more acceptable and effective behavioral outcomes and prevent future transgressions.

Emotion Coaching is a relational approach, not a behavioral approach

We're all familiar with the common use of rewards and sanctions to modify behavior. Perhaps your setting or school uses reward charts or detentions, or even exclusion to control behavior. These kinds of strategies focus on the behavior, rather than their underlying causes. The use of rewards and sanctions is based on the premise that behavior can be controlled and modified via positive and negative reinforcement and usually translated into systems of rewards and sanctions. Hence, they are usually referred to as "behavioral" approaches (although the work of Skinner (1953) on whose work these systems are based is often misinterpreted).

An assumption underpinning behavioral approaches is that children are in control of their behavior and can make a conscious choice about their reactions to an event. However, our understanding about emotional development and more recent theories about our "upstairs" and "downstairs" brains (Siegel and Payne Bryson, 2012) suggest that children experiencing strong emotions may not be making a rational choice about their behavior.

A behavioral approach relies not only on children's capacity to envisage and understand the consequences of their behavior, but also a desire and ability to delay gratification or regulate innate emotional needs—abilities that may not have yet developed in some children. There are also vulnerable children, whose priority to feel safe and secure overwhelms any capacity to respond to a behavior management system that relies on a fully functioning rational mind. Thus, challenging or unregulated behavior may reflect a difficulty in understanding and managing the emotional response linked to an event, rather than choice. Continuing to sanction behavior does nothing to support a child's ability to understand the feeling that underpins the behavior, and so the behavior continues to be displayed (Parker, Rose and Gilbert, 2016). This is reflected in the growing numbers of fixed and permanent exclusions in the UK (Parker *et al.*, 2016).

Primary school teachers and parents will know that the lure of "stickers" often wears off after a while. And putting a child's name on the "dark cloud" doesn't seem to deter some more challenging behaviour, even becoming a badge of honour for some. Secondary teachers will know the pupils for whom detention does not always seem to act as a sufficient deterrent or who have no desire to win an award and continue to break the rules. For some children, the reward and sanction system fails to support or guide their behavior and is insufficient to help them regulate their feelings and learn new ways of behaving (Rose, McGuire-Snieckus and Gilbert, 2019).

Although behavioral approaches dominate school behavior management policies, schools are increasingly realizing that relational approaches can work just as effectively. Indeed, they can go further by reaching those children for whom rewards and sanctions just do not work (Gus *et al.*, 2017). Here is an example of a three-year-old in a nursery where Emotion Coaching seemed to work more effectively than a reward and sanction approach.

The early years practitioners had used the "time out" system and whenever the child had a tantrum, which was frequently, they put his name on the "sad face" board and put him in the "time out chair." He would often resist and continue to scream, for up to an hour, until he was exhausted. The staff felt fraught and often his screaming upset the other children. After staff were trained in Emotion Coaching, the "sad face" chart was taken down as they recognized that publicly shaming a three-year-old may not be the most effective way to help him learn to self-regulate. The "time out chair" was renamed and changed into a more comfortable "calming chair." The practitioners could now sit with the child when he "flipped his lid," and soothed and empathized with him until he was calmer. They could then talk with him about his feelings using emoji cards and encourage him to go to the calming chair when he felt frustrated. Although it took about three months of consistently using Emotion Coaching before this child fully stopped his tantrum behavior, the practitioners immediately noticed that using an Emotion Coaching approach calmed him down much more quickly and the frequency of the tantrums diminished within a week.

Emotion Coaching is a relational approach which develops internal regulations

- External Frameworks
- External Regulation

- Internal Frameworks
- Internal Regulation

Sanctions and Rewards
Behavioural Management Policy

Emotion Coaching
Behavior-Regulation Policy

FIGURE 2.2. BEHAVIORAL VS RELATIONAL APPROACHES (© EMOTION COACHING UK)

A relational approach works with the child's internal regulatory systems to soothe and calm so that the brain and body are more receptive to hearing school rules and to rational and reasonable problem-solving.

Some educational settings have shifted their thinking about behavior and are developing school policies aimed at promoting the development of emotional and behavioral regulation through co-regulation rather than managing pupil behavior (Gus *et al.*, 2017). These are relational behavior policies, or self-regulation policies (Ahmed, 2018), acknowledging that self-regulation is a skill that needs to be practiced and learned over time. For example, we spend years teaching children to read and write, accepting that they will make mistakes along the way, and we provide extra support for those that are finding this skill more difficult to achieve. The underlying belief with a relational approach such as Emotion Coaching is that children might not be able to understand or manage the emotions that are giving rise to their behavior in a particular context. However, with the support of an attuned adult, they will be able to develop this understanding and then regulate their emotions, and so improve their behavior. They are more receptive to alternative ways of behaving and become empowered to regulate themselves sufficiently so that they can engage with school rules and learning.

One particularly interesting outcome from our research was the reduced need for and frequent use of rewards and sanctions by one secondary school once Emotion Coaching was adopted as a strategy (Rose, Gilbert and McGuire-Snieckus, 2015). This evidence implies that focusing attention on the underlying feelings of the behavior rather than just on modifying the behavior helps to reduce the need for rewards and sanctions as a means of changing behavior.

Emotion Coaching is very much a relational approach. As we saw earlier in this chapter, Emotion Coaching promotes positive relationships, generating safety and trust between the adult and child through empathic communication.

Disapproving, dismissing and laissez-faire approaches

Another way to distinguish the particular features of Emotion Coaching is to understand what it is not. When Gottman and his colleagues (1997) undertook their initial research and identified Emotion Coaching parents, they also noticed other ways parents engaged with their children's emotions. They found three other natural parenting styles.

Disapproving style

A "disapproving" approach to behavior management views emotions as a sign of weakness or a lack of personal control. A "disapproving" adult lacks empathy and may be critical and intolerant of emotional displays. They try to banish difficult emotions by using discipline, reprimand or punishment. A "disapproving" practitioner focuses on the behavior of the child rather than the emotions generating the behavior. In this kind of response, emotional displays from children are viewed as a form of manipulation, a lack of obedience or a sign of bad character. Behavior management strategies are motivated by a need to control or regain power or to "toughen up" the child and are commonly expressed with an assertive, stern and angry tone. Although they may appear successful in the short term, with a disapproving style the adult is modeling an angry response. This is probably the least effective way of developing a child's emotional understanding or trusting relationships.

Dismissing style

A "dismissing" style of behavior management can be well intended but is often driven by a desire to make things better and minimize distress by ignoring the emotions, trying to make them better using distraction or other techniques. Dismissing adults can view emotions and children's emotional displays as trivial or unimportant. Emotions such as anger and sadness need to be "got over quickly." This kind of adult considers that paying attention to such emotions will make them worse and so prolong the emotional state. Therefore, a "dismissing" adult doesn't engage with a child's emotions and will try to stop emotions by ignoring, minimizing or "making light" of their importance. They may rely on logic and distraction or reward to try and help a child feel better. Common phrases might be "Don't worry about it," 'Be a big girl," "It's okay, you'll be fine," "Hey, let's have a biscuit" and "Let's play with this toy instead." Problem-solving doesn't occur.

It is important to distinguish a dismissing style from a disapproving style as it often appears to be a warmer and more empathic response. Indeed, it is often motivated by a desire to rescue and help the child. Gottman and colleagues (1997) noted that this style was the most common parenting style and our research found it to be the most common practitioner style (Rose, Gilbert and McGuire-Snieckus, 2015). Although a dismissing style is gentler and less dictatorial than an disapproving style, it does not allow the child to engage with how and why they are feeling in a particular way.

Laissez-faire style

This style may be driven by empathy and understanding, freely accepting all emotional expression and readily providing comfort to a child experiencing difficult feelings. However, it offers little guidance and does not teach the child about their emotions or how to manage them. It adopts a permissive style without setting limits or helping the child to solve problems. There's a sense that emotions need to be "ridden out" or "let out" with little that can be done about them. To the laissez-faire practitioner, difficult and challenging emotions are a simple matter of hydraulics—release the emotion and the work is done. So, like dismissive practitioners, laissez-faire practitioners might appear warm and have good intentions, but no boundaries are set and no problem-solving is explored to improve regulation. There is, therefore, little engagement with the child's feelings and a child is, in essence, left to "cry it out" rather than being co-regulated and learning helpful self-soothing strategies. Children experiencing this style are likely to grow up unprepared for challenges, with fewer strategies to cope with life's ups and downs.

The impact of emotion dismissing, disapproving and laissez-faire approaches

Although dismissing, disapproval and laissez-faire approaches can often work and temporarily stop unacceptable behaviour, children experiencing these styles of interaction do not necessarily learn to understand and trust what they are feeling, or distinguish between feelings and behaviors. The message they deliver to the children is that what they are feeling is not normal, "not right," and that their assessment is wrong and they should not feel this way. This can lead to children feeling isolated and as if no one is helping them. The suppression of innate and natural emotions, which are replaced by unrestrained dysregulation or a reliance on distraction or reward to reduce the intensity of the feeling.

Since they are not given opportunities to experience emotions and to learn about them, they may generate more unhelpful emotions such as shame and resentment. An example of how a non-Emotion Coaching style can foster resentment in children came from a discussion with 15-year-old Izzy:

> *Izzy was annoyed because she had worn the incorrect jumper to PE and her PE teacher had given her two options: take the jumper off or sit out the lesson. These two options were consistently presented to Izzy by the teacher as she protested that it was cold, and she wanted to play netball. Eventually, Izzy sat down and observed the lesson without making a fuss. The teacher may have thought, "Success! I was firm, consistent and ended up with a good result, I'll use that approach again!" Wrong! As Izzy sat there watching the lesson, she was seething with anger and resentment, "Look at the teacher, she is wearing a warm hoodie and fleecy track pants; she isn't cold but she was prepared for me to be cold. So unfair!" Izzy and her PE teacher continued to have a fractious and confrontational relationship.*

Dismissing, disapproving and Emotion Coaching are approaches mostly favoured by adults in responding to emotional displays in children. This is reflected in the story of Matthew, a case study from our original pilot research (Rose, Gilbert and McGuire-Snieckus, 2015):

> *Matthew was a nine-year-old who was suspected of having attention deficit hyperactive disorder as he found it hard to focus on his schoolwork and was easily distracted. He was described as often needing to be stimulated by new things and he liked taking risks. This became more apparent during break time where he would often flout the school rules by trying out new adventures such as climbing on the wall. There were three supervisors who supported and monitored the children during the lunch break. The supervisors' responses to Matthew's challenging behavior reflected three of the*

styles identified by Gottman: disapproving, dismissing and a natural Emotion Coaching approach.

The school described how the disapproving supervisor tended to get cross with Matthew when he did something wrong such as climbing on the low wall. She would "tell him off" and show her disapproval for him breaking the rules, even when he hurt himself by falling off the wall.

The dismissive supervisor would tend to try to play down displays of emotions and use personally directed humour, and even sarcasm, when commenting on his behavior ("typical boy," "come on, you're not a baby" type expressions) and ignore any distress.

The Emotion Coaching supervisor connected with him emotionally by saying that she understood why he wanted to do what he did, but that they all had to follow the playground rules, so they needed to figure out what other ways were safe for everyone. The way she communicated was empathic and validated his sensory-seeking needs but still made it clear what the boundaries were. She was also able to talk with Matthew about how he felt when he wanted to do "fun but dangerous things" and work with him to find some safer, but equally stimulating, games he could play instead.

What was noticeable from this case study was that Matthew was more responsive to the Emotion Coaching supervisor. He more readily followed her instructions, was less likely to exhibit risk-taking behavior in her presence and happily joined in the games with her. When the other supervisors attempted to play the games with him, he was either reluctant or refused.

This story suggests that through Emotion Coaching the supervisor was able to build a trusting relationship with Matthew, and so was able to help him to manage constructively the challenges of the playground.

Co-regulation

A key process involved in Emotion Coaching is co-regulation. By empathizing with a child's emotional state, even when they are displaying inappropriate behavior, we are providing an in-the-moment relational support structure for that child to calm down and learn to self-regulate. We readily provide support structures to scaffold all other aspects of children's learning. For example, we help children learn to talk by talking with them—this narrative helps children to engage, understand and respond and begin to articulate their own words. With Emotion Coaching, we are providing a similar scaffold and narrative for them to learn about their own emotions and how they can be regulated. Co-regulation involves working with another person to help them to regulate their feelings and behavior. It involves warm, responsive interactions which provide support, coaching and modeling to help others understand, express and regulate their feelings, behavior and thoughts. Emotion Coaching is a co-regulating strategy as it operates like a scaffold that supports another by helping them to learn to calm down.

Once again, we can turn to some recent neuroscientific evidence to help us understand how important co-regulation is in helping children to self-regulate and to develop better vagal tone. You may recall from the previous chapter how vagal tone plays an important part in helping us to regulate stress. Gottman's (1997) research showed that Emotion Coaching appears to have an effective impact on the operation of the vagus nerve, suggesting that the techniques help trigger the vagus nerve into assisting the brain and body to calm down. Repeated experiences of co-regulation enable children to improve their vagal tone.

Good vagal tone appears to directly benefit our wellbeing and responses to stress in later life (Porges, 2011). While children's brains and nervous systems are still under construction, it is particularly important for practitioners and parents to help support children in developing good vagal tone. Gottman and DeClaire (1997) provide a useful metaphor to explain this—they comment that just as children with good muscle tone do well in sporting activities, children who have good vagal tone are better at responding to and recovering from emotional stress.

Modeling empathy

The issue of adults' modeling appropriate emotional responses becomes particularly significant when we consider the relatively recent neuroscientific discovery of the mirroring system. You will recall from Chapter 1 that this mirroring system is activated by simply watching others perform intentional actions and when we copy others' actions. Thus, the mirroring system appears to enable us to mimic the behavior of others, perhaps priming us to be able to replicate behaviors to communicate with others. In relation to behavior management, some neuroscientists consider that the mirroring system provides the building blocks for empathy and socialization by building our capacity to emulate others and understand others' intent (LePage and Theoret, 2007).

Therefore, if we are trying to support a child who has pushed another child and we respond to them with an angry expression and tone of voice as well as finger wagging, the mirroring system in the child's brain is likely to try to emulate the same response. This is exactly the opposite of what we wish to convey to an already angry and dysregulated child. Instead, by modeling a calmer, more empathic response to the child's emotional state, more empathic behaviors will be fostered. In this way, we help the child to understand the need to inhibit their immediate desire to push another child, and to develop more prosocial engagement. In other words, we need to experience empathy in order to be empathic.

Baron-Cohen (2011) suggests empathy requires effective personal recognition and response skills and is a complex process that has different dimensions which are still not fully understood. Empathy can be categorized as affective, cognitive and compassionate.

Affective, or emotional, empathy is being able to share a feeling in another through an emotional connection. Cognitive empathy relates to our ability to understand how another might be feeling and thinking. Compassionate empathy involves having a desire to take action to help support another (Baron-Cohen, 2011; Goleman, 2007).

We suggest that Emotion Coaching is a suitable vehicle to develop skills in recognizing and responding empathically. It promotes the three dimensions of empathy through recognizing how a child is feeling (affective empathy), understanding their perspective and validating their experience (cognitive empathy) and then working with the other to help them (compassionate empathy).

The messages of Emotion Coaching

The messages children receive when they experience an Emotion Coaching style is that we all have feelings, that they are all natural and normal. These feelings inform our wishes and desires, which are also normal. However, they may need to be regulated and expressed constructively and not all our wishes and desires may be met. It conveys to the child that they are not alone, that they are accepted, supported, valid, cared for, understood, trusted and respected.

Emotion Coaching supports children's learning by encouraging them to feel calm and safe enough to engage in their own problem-solving. Thus, through Emotion Coaching, a child learns to empathize, to read others' emotions and social cues, to control impulses, self-sooth and self-regulate, to delay gratification, to motivate themselves and to cope with life's ups and downs (to be resilient). It also shows children how conflicts might be resolved peacefully through self-control, and builds problem-solving capacity and wellbeing.

We saw previously how Siegel (2012) has highlighted the importance of communication and integration within different parts of the brain and the body in order to develop and sustain wellbeing. Emotion Coaching seems to be particularly effective, not only in soothing the limbic system and the stress response, but also in enabling adults to help children to connect and reconnect the limbic system to the frontal lobes. This then allows them to be able to process experiences in an integrated way.

Emotion Coaching provides the adult with an effective strategy to help children learn to self-regulate their emotions and consequently their behaviour by:

- triggering a calmer response through empathic support

- co-regulating children to assist self-soothing through raising their awareness of their own emotional state and helping them to establish good vagal tone

- using the emotional moment as an opportunity to scaffold the children's self-management of their emotions and behavior.

Emotion Coaching promotes young children's self-awareness of emotions and positive self-regulation of their behaviour, and generates more nurturing relationships. In nurturing relationships, young children can feel protected, comforted and secure within a context of caring and trustworthy adults, who support them in their emotional self-regulation. As one practitioner put it,

"It makes the children feel more secure and gives them a vocabulary to talk about how they are feeling instead of just acting out. This helps them to be more positive and happier."

Chapter 3

How to Emotion Coach

The four steps of Emotion Coaching

In this chapter, we're going to look at how you actually "do" Emotion Coaching. You may remember that Emotion Coaching was identified by John Gottman and his colleagues as consisting of the following features: being aware of a child's response; recognizing emotional times as opportunities for intimacy and teaching; listening empathically and validating the child's feelings; helping the child to verbally label emotions, and setting limits; and helping the child to problem-solve. During our research we found that for busy adults, it is helpful to translate these processes into a set of four steps:

Step 1: Recognizing the child's feelings and empathizing with them.

Step 2: Labeling the feelings and validating them.

Step 3: Setting limits on behavior if needed.

Step 4: Problem-solving with the child.

As will be explained as we work through each of the Emotion

Coaching steps, it may not always be appropriate or necessary for all the steps to be completed in the moment nor always delivered in order. You need to be able to make a realistic appraisal of the emotional moment for the child and the context to determine the number and sequence of steps. However, we emphasize that Steps 1 and 2 are a priority and seen as a necessity to help support a child to calm down.

This is because, in recognizing, understanding and empathically engaging with a child, you "attune" to their emotional needs, fostering a sense of being seen and feeling safe. In moments of distress, an attuned relationship between an adult and child can influence and organize the mind of the child to regulate themselves in the moment, to develop their regulatory capacity and acquire skills for use in the future (Schore, 2000). Attuned relationships involve knowing when a child needs your mental and perhaps physical support and when they need to be alone. Therefore, at the root of attunement is an adult's ability to read verbal and non-verbal signals indicating a child's needs, and the tools and skill to respond and support appropriately. Emotion Coaching's four steps can be seen as a vehicle to deliver, as well as a way for adults to sustain, attuned relationships.

Step 1: Recognize and empathize

Be a detective rather than a judge

The first step of Emotion Coaching is about noticing what is happening to the child. Look beyond their actions to recognize the emotions that may be driving the behavior. What is the child feeling in that moment? Behavior is a form of communication— something has happened, or is about to, that is making the child feel an emotion. An iceberg metaphor (Figure 3.1) can help to explain this: imagine that the behavior you are seeing is the tip of an iceberg and that beneath, hidden from us, lies a much bigger mass of ice. Don't assume that the child's behavior reveals the whole story. The behavior is being driven by a complicated mass of underlying emotions. The emotions give rise to the behavior, so for us to support the child, we need to try and uncover those emotions lying beneath.

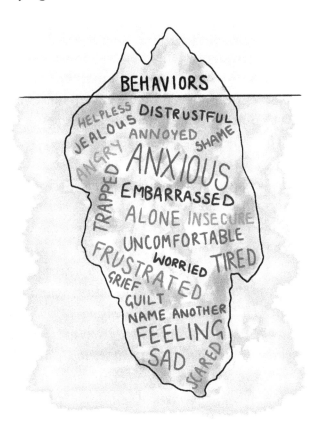

FIGURE 3.1 THE FEELINGS ICEBERG

Rather than acting as a judge of whether the behavior is right or wrong, think of yourself as a detective. Are there any clues to help you understand what emotion the child is feeling? You might look for physical or non-verbal signs of the emotion being felt, after all, much of our communication is non-verbal. Notice facial expression, body tone, gestures and posture. Has the child become lethargic and floppy? Has the child's face gone red, are their eyebrows furrowed or their lips pursed? Has their body stiffened? Have they lowered their eyes? Non-verbal cues give us information about which emotions are being felt and about their intensity, which provides meaning and context.

Think also about the situation the child is in right now. From your perspective, you may feel the child is overreacting or behaving inappropriately, but what might be causing this particular child to feel so challenged? It's important to be able to take on the child's point of view by putting yourself in their shoes.

Joanne, a specialist support teacher, recalls:

I observed a young person on arrival at the pupil referral unit; he sat in a ball, with his hood up, by the door in the entrance area. One staff member attempted to gently coax him into the form room but he reacted by swearing and kicking at the wall and door. He became increasingly agitated as the staff member encouraged him to join the class group, and bunched himself further into a corner and repeatedly kicked at the wall and increased his swearing.

The young person had a history of anxiety at leaving home and I could empathize that pupil referral unit settings can feel intimidating due to the emotional needs of other students. While the young man was displaying some physical aggression, I felt that this was to drive adults away. I felt that his primary emotions were fear and anxiety about entering his form group. He was staying by the door to communicate that he didn't want to be there and wished to be at home.

Building a power base

When a child is experiencing strong, difficult emotions, soothing is the priority. This emotional first aid helps the child to feel calmer and so become more responsive to direction, allowing their thinking to re-engage with the rational or "upstairs" part of their brain. Indeed, Gottman and DeClaire (1997, p.120) believe that "to propose solutions before you empathize with children is like trying to build the frame of a house before you lay a firm foundation." Many other specialists also recognize and advocate the importance of adults building an emotional bond with children, and the need to show empathy. A number of catch phrases help remind us of these requirements and urge us to resist jumping in to set limits and problem-solve. Siegel (Siegel and Payne Bryson, 2012, p.22) thinks that parents should "connect and re-direct," Riley (2010) suggests that teachers should establish rapport before they try to reason with pupils, and Golding (2015, p.152) urges "connection before correction."

Julia, an educational psychologist, reports the following inter-action and conversation with a 14-year-old. This highlights how an empathic response enabled a connection to be made, and from this came acceptance by the young person of the boundaries of the situation:

> I had been warned by the staff that Hayley "wouldn't last more than 20 minutes." Nevertheless, the school was keen that I assessed Hayley and provided them with a report. I felt under tremendous pressure. I had never met this girl before, she would only last 20 minutes maximum before walking out and I had to somehow write a report at the end of this. Hayley came in, sat down and gave monosyllabic answers to my initial get to know you questions. Tension started to mount in me, and I was conscious of the clock ticking in the room—every tick was one closer to the point when Hayley would leave the room. I asked Hayley how she slept. Hayley mentioned that she couldn't sleep. I asked Hayley what time she did get to sleep and Hayley said usually about 5am every morning... Short pause in real time, long pause in my brain... I saw

this as my Emotion Coaching, or rather empathy, moment. I didn't have to judge and respond in a disapproving manner by commenting on whether going to sleep at 5am was a good thing or bad thing or suggesting that as most young people are on their phones all night, how could she expect to get to sleep. Rather than ignoring the sleep issue and moving through my interview protocol, or responding in an emotion-dismissing manner by mentioning that maybe she was exaggerating a little and must get to sleep before that time, I made myself stop and consider my response. I thought about not being able to get to sleep until 5am myself and how that makes me feel in the morning. I said, "Oh, it must be so hard to get up in the mornings then for school if you don't get to sleep until 5am." Hayley looked at me directly for the first time, we talked more about her sleep and after about ten seconds or so of empathic talk about her sleep, Hayley finished with, "My foster carer doesn't believe me about this."

The interview was then transformed. Hayley started talking to me, her posture improved, eye contact improved, and she started genuinely interacting with me. The 20 minutes went by, then an hour had passed; after 90 minutes I asked Hayley whether she wanted a break but she told me she was fine. After two and a half hours, we had completed a really good piece of assessment including a comprehensive assessment of phonics which Hayley found incredibly difficult and challenging. Hayley even managed to giggle over the sounds she couldn't say.

Emotional first aid

Your initial response when a child is moaning, snatching equipment from another child or refusing to get dressed for PE may be to think, "Things are never right for her," "I wish they'd stop doing that" or "He's going slow on purpose." Rather than reacting to the behavior you see, remember that the first step of Emotion Coaching suggests you put yourself in the child's shoes in that moment. What might the child be feeling that causes them to behave like that and what is the situation that causes the child to feel like that? Are they frustrated with writing because their working memory is easily overloaded? Are they nervous because of a change in today's timetable, or unsure about what is happening next? Are they worried because they're starting a new school soon?

We need to be able to be genuine in our empathy, as we can all detect when someone does not mean it. Children can tell if we are not being genuinely empathic. Remember that feeling empathy with the child does not mean you agree with or condone their behavior. Feelings give rise to the behavior and identifying and empathizing with the feelings is different to approving of the behavior that arose as a consequence.

By being empathic, you are better able to establish an attuned connection with the child. This connection enables you to support the child through co-regulation. As discussed in Chapter 1, once a child experiences an empathic response from those around them, their social engagement system and vagus nerve are more likely to be activated, helping to generate a calming response in their brain, mind and body. Being empathic gives emotional first aid that can help children to feel safer and creates a kind of "safe haven," a place of trust, acceptance and respect. From this emotional base, children are often more willing and able to return respect and accept boundaries and rules.

Empathy sounds easy and straightforward, but it can be difficult to generate and communicate. When our own difficult emotions become activated in response to the child's display of emotions, we ourselves may respond with reactive language or behavior. When you repeatedly hear a child saying, "Miss, I don't know what I have to do" and you have explained it three times already, your exasperated response might be "I've told you three times but you've chosen not to listen, now, get on with your work!" However, in the following example, the teacher, Aisha, takes the time to consider what the child might be feeling and what emotional first aid may be needed:

> *Nine-year-old Freddy was not following instructions in class. He crawled under the table with some Lego when it was time to start writing. Aisha wondered if he may be feeling sad because he seemed quieter than usual that day. She went over to him, bent down, and looked kindly at him. She spoke softly, "Hey Freddy, I'll sit here with you for a bit."*

Putting yourself in the child's shoes

As we have mentioned earlier, being able to put yourself in the child's shoes is essentially what the first step of Emotion Coaching is all about. The psychologist Elizabeth Meins and her colleagues have showed how important it is for parents to treat their children as "persons with thoughts and feeling," and this process is called being "mind-minded" (Meins *et al.*, 2001). Mind-mindedness is more than just being sensitive to your child's needs. It involves active engagement with the child and accepting that the child has their own mind. It's about attuning with and reflecting on what is really going on in the child's mind. Fonagy and his colleagues (2004) refer to the process of perceiving, interpreting and attending to the mental state of others by understanding their needs, desires, feelings, beliefs and interests as mentalization. They emphasize how important mentalizing is to support healthy emotional development in children.

Emotion Coaching involves mind-mindedness and mentalization. The steps of Emotion Coaching enable attunement to the child and support adult mentalization about a child (Rose, Gilbert and McGuire-Snieckus, 2015). In turn, this supports the child's ability to develop their own mind-mindedness and abilities to mentalize. Through Emotion Coaching's attunement, we can convey to children our understanding and acceptance of their emotional state.

In a primary school for children with additional learning needs, Maria, a teaching assistant, highlights attunement and mentalization in her interaction with Sam:

Maria was supporting Sam, one to one, in class during science. Sam didn't want to do any more work so Maria reminded Sam that there were only a few more minutes to go and used a sand timer as a visual cue. Previously, Sam had responded to this prompt, but not on this occasion; Sam swore at Maria, charged out of class and ran along the corridor pulling over wheelchairs and walking frames.

Maria calmly followed Sam along the corridor keeping her distance but helping him to feel safe with her presence. She continued to observe Sam closely, looking and listening for subtle changes in his body language and breathing. After a minute, Maria sensed a decrease in intensity of emotion and began to use empathic communication, "It's okay, Sam, I know that maths made you really angry and maybe you felt I didn't listen to you." Sam shouted, "I hate science." Maria paused and replied, "Yes, I can hear that was tough for you. How about we go sit on our bean bags for a bit?" Sam looked at her for the first time and said, "I don't wanna sit on a bean bag." Maria accepted his choice and suggested, "Okay, you don't fancy the bean bag right now. Come on, let's get ourselves out of this corridor, go and chill for a bit and pop some bubble wrap and have a drink." Sam moved a little closer and nodded.

Maria and Sam went to their chill-out area, sat on a bean bag and popped some bubble wrap, Sam sucked cold water hard through a curly straw (helping to trigger an early years soothing reflex) and his body began to slump while his face became less flushed.

We can see Steps 1 and 2 of Emotion Coaching in the above interaction: being aware of the child's emotional state, empathizing with it and then labeling and validating the emotions.

Sam calmed down enough to return to the classroom but quickly lost his temper again when it was time to pack up and get ready to go home. He continued in the following manner:

Sam: I'm not clearing up!

Maria: You sound like you're cross thinking you have to clear up?

Sam: Yes, you always make me clear up.

Maria: Sounds like you don't like clearing up?

Sam: I hate it, it's not my job.

Maria: Hmmm.

From this exchange, Maria understood that Sam was still cross and was still in a heightened state of arousal. She recognized this was not the right time to begin limit-setting, problem-solving and repairing what went wrong. At this stage, Sam needed further co-regulation to reduce his emotional arousal levels:

Maria handed Sam a stress ball and suggested that they try to do some big breaths together. Maria was aware that Sam could be resistant to deep breathing with an adult as sometimes he didn't want to calm down at the adult's pace. However, having been in a very physical and highly aroused state for a longer time than usual, Sam welcomed the comfort and routine of big breaths. Maria then read Sam a favourite book and they both sat together on the bean bag. Following the deep breathing, stress ball, book reading and close contact, Sam was physically calmer, and Maria felt able to restart the Emotion Coaching conversation: "So what happened, Sam? What was it about science this morning?" Sam was then able to explain and

*understand that he didn't follow what was going on in the lesson and
what was being said to him.*

Through continued reflections on Sam's internal state, displayed
by his behavior, Maria was able to attune herself to his emotional
state. Sam was able to experience a mind that had him in mind
rather than one that overwhelmed him (Fonagy and Target,
1998). These attuned interpersonal experiences contribute to the
development of emotional regulation skills. Maria conveyed her
understanding of Sam's emotional state by moving through and
then looping back on various steps of Emotion Coaching as needed.

Helping yourself to be more empathic

When a child behaves in a way that is challenging, it is easy to
revert to the familiar ways of dealing with the behavior with repri-
mands so that the child will "learn." However, if the child does not
understand the feeling that caused the behavior, how are they to
learn? The more we practice responding in an empathic rather than
judgemental way to inappropriate behavior, the easier it becomes.

Lisa, an educational psychologist, recalled a conversation with
a mother, Debra, about her daughter missing out on half a sausage
and Debra missing out on a trip to Paris. The scenarios were different but the emotions experienced were similar. By supporting
Debra to think of an equivalent adult situation, Lisa supported the
mother to empathize with her daughter:

*Debra described her eight-year-old daughter Hattie as "ruining
family life." Debra recounted an event when the family had invited
another family to join them on a Friday night. The plan was for the
children to play together and for the adults to engage in conversation.
As part of this planned, relaxed end to the week, the parents decided
to order takeaway food for dinner. When it was time to order the*

food, Debra asked Hattie what she would like; "A battered sausage" was the response.

When the food arrived home, Debra started to plate out the children's food. Debra got to Hattie's plate and, remembering that Hattie had had an upset tummy the day before, decided to give Hattie half the sausage and half of the fish her son had ordered. She reasoned that the battered sausage contained a lot of fat and Hattie quite liked fish. On being given her plate, Hattie got angry and threw the plate against the wall, yelling, "Where's my battered sausage? I hate you! Where's my battered sausage?"

Hattie continued to rage, despite Debra explaining that Hattie hadn't been feeling very well the previous day, and that the sausage might upset her tummy so, as she liked fish, it was a good compromise to ensure that she would continue to enjoy the evening playing with her family and friends. Hattie refused to listen and continued to yell and scream. Debra started to feel embarrassed that she could not control her eight-year-old daughter and told Hattie to go to her room to calm down. Hattie refused, and feeling angry, annoyed and embarrassed, Debra took Hattie to her room, but Hattie repeatedly returned to the kitchen screaming that she wanted her battered sausage and how she hated her mother. As Debra recounted this story, her anger and embarrassment were evident.

Lisa thought about the emotions that Hattie might have felt when she did not receive what she had anticipated and asked Debra if she had ever experienced an occasion when she was really looking forward to something and it had not materialized. After some thought, Debra recalled an occasion when she and her partner had planned to go to Paris for a long weekend. She had never been to Paris before and was really looking forward to the weekend away with just her partner. On the day of departure, Debra, with her bag ready at the front door, was waiting for her partner to arrive home from work. However, when he got home Debra's partner simply said, "Sorry Debra, we can't go, I have to work this weekend." As Debra *related her story, she appeared to become angry and irritated. Lisa said, "Oh, you must have felt really let down and disappointed as you were so looking forward to the trip." Debra started to agree with Lisa, then stopped herself as she suddenly realized and said, "Oh, it's the same as the battered sausage, isn't it?"*

After she put herself in her daughter's shoes and viewed the situation from her daughter's perspective rather than judging the situation by her own adult standards—"it's only a sausage!"—Debra attuned empathically with Hattie. Her perceptions of Hattie's behaviour changed from annoyance and anger to an understanding of how Hattie might be feeling when she displayed challenging behaviour, and so she improved her support for Hattie to understand and manage those feelings.

The challenges of empathy

Our experience of assisting teachers, practitioners and parents with Emotion Coaching to support the development of children's emotional understanding has frequently highlighted some aspects of communication that can interfere with responding empathically to children experiencing difficult emotions. Let's take a look at them.

We can feel empathy but might communicate dismissively

Adults may know and understand how a child is feeling in a particular situation but their style of response to these emotions might not show acknowledgement or actually label them. If the adult's response simply tries to make the difficult emotion go away for the child, they can become dismissive. We have said, in the previous chapter, how the work of Gottman and colleagues (1997) identified this as the most common parenting style (dismissive). We have found, in our studies, that practitioners, in an attempt to keep control of the situation and do it quickly, can also be dismissive, but that with practice can adopt a more Emotion Coaching approach (Rose, Gilbert and McGuire-Snieckus, 2015).

An example of this is highlighted in a conversation with Claudia, mother to two young boys (aged five and seven years), and her friend Karen:

Claudia and her partner had separated, and the boys' father was living full time with a new partner who had two girls of about the same age as the boys. The boys saw their father for six days every fortnight. Claudia had become concerned with the boys' behavior when they returned home from the visits to their father's new home. They were often sullen, irritable with one another and defiant with her. Claudia felt that she understood that the boys' behavior reflected their worries that their father would start to love the girls more than he loved them. To Karen, this seemed a well-attuned understanding of how the boys might be feeling and she suggested to Claudia that the boys might find an empathic response supportive.

Claudia said, "Oh, I did empathy, it didn't work." Karen asked Claudia to try and explain. Claudia said that when the boys came home they seemed down and glum and so she tried to reassure them by saying "Don't worry, Daddy still loves you." The boys responded by yelling, "Shut up Mummy, don't use those words with us." The younger boy went to his room and broke some toys, while the older son did not speak to her for several days. "See, empathy doesn't work," Claudia said.

Karen asked Claudia if her response had shown her children that she could see that they were worried and insecure right now or whether it had tried to put an end to the children's difficult emotions? Claudia said that she now realized that perhaps she felt distressed and powerless by her children's display of feelings and had ended up ignoring their emotions—because she wanted her sons to know their father did love them. In doing so, she had forgotten to show and acknowledge that she recognized and understood their feelings of worry and insecurity.

In her desire to cheer her boys, inadvertently, Claudia had acted dismissively. Her sons had no idea that their mother understood how they were feeling, and her choice of words added to their sense that she indeed had no understanding. The boys' language in response to Claudia's attempts to ease their feelings of insecurity and fear suggests this may well have been the case.

We think empathy suggests we agree with a behavior

In this book, we suggest that behavior is often the result of a "felt emotion" and that "learning" about emotions develops through our relationships with others. Yet, historically, Western culture has a long tradition of focusing attention only on behavior, and the most prevalent way to develop behavior is to reward or punish—the assumption is that children can be coerced to learn to behave. This behaviorist approach is based on the idea that behavior results from rational cognitive decision-making and that emotions play very little part in the process. Interestingly, however, the evidence of rewards and sanctions as deterrents of behavior is relatively weak and often misapplied (Parker *et al.*, 2016).

Behavioral ways of thinking can be strong and natural for many of us, so trying to think differently about the role of emotions in behavior can be challenging. We all know how hard it is to change thinking and habits (Baumeister and Vohs, 2004) and this is illustrated in the following example.

Towards the end of an Emotion Coaching training session at a secondary school, Mike, a deputy headteacher, commented that he agreed with the rationale behind Emotion Coaching and could see how it might be of benefit to the pupils in the school. However, he added that sometimes it would not be possible to be empathic, preventing him using Emotion Coaching. The example Mike gave related to a discussion about how Emotion Coaching could have been used with Lila, a 14-year-old pupil:

> *Lila was on a final warning for aggressive behavior and had thrown a chair across the art room. She had become angry because she had been told that she couldn't participate in the up and coming art show. In throwing the chair she had destroyed some art work and injured the teacher. She had been sent to see Mike, who told her that this was the final straw and she was now going to be permanently excluded. Lila showed no remorse at her actions and was still angry. Mike said, "I couldn't have been empathic with this pupil. I could not have said, yes, I would have thrown the table too if I'd been in your shoes."*

Mike's comments show how important it is to understand attunement in Emotion Coaching. Attunement is about recognizing and empathizing with the emotion, not the behavior. The behavior, throwing a table across the room, was unacceptable, but what was the emotion driving the behavior? Mike could have had empathy for the fact that Lila was furious about a perceived injustice in the way she was being treated—she believed other pupils would not have been excluded. An empathic response, acknowledging her anger, could have promoted an attuned connection to help trigger the vagus nerve to calm her state of stress and support her self-regulation. Empathizing does not preclude the consequences of unacceptable behavior nor does it condone improper conduct, but if we are trying to change behavior, punishments alone are not necessarily the most effective tool.

Sympathy versus empathy

Sympathy and empathy can be easily confused as both relate to the relationship a person has with the feelings and experiences of another. However, they differ in a crucial way that is critical to Emotion Coaching.

Sympathy is largely used to communicate commiseration, pity, or feelings of sorrow for someone else who is experiencing misfortune; you feel bad for them, but you don't conceive what it is like to be in their shoes. It is more detached than empathy and doesn't involve taking on another's view by imagining their emotions.

Empathy refers to the capacity to imagine yourself in the situation of another, relating to the experience, understanding and feeling with the emotions, ideas, or opinions of that person. Sympathy might convey concern and can lead to a more empathic response, but it often lacks clear evidence to communicate to the other your willingness to accept and ability to support a shared perspective or a shared emotion.

Luke, an educational psychologist, writes of a consultation with Katie, a mother of two children both with additional educational needs. Luke had known Katie for several years through his involvement with Katie's eldest child Jack. Jack was ten years old and had previously been diagnosed with autism spectrum condition/attention deficit hyperactivity disorder. Jack rarely had positive social interactions at school, either with pupils or teachers. Jack's long-standing difficulty with social interaction is poignantly illustrated by the fact that he had never been invited to another child's birthday party:

On this occasion, I met with Katie again as part of a review meeting for her daughter who needed additional support for literacy. At the end of the meeting, Katie asked whether she could have a word with me about Jack. Katie told me that Jack had made a really good start to the school year. His new class teacher seemed to really understand him and had been able to help with some of the difficulties with social interactions as and when they occurred. As a result, Jack was feeling that he could trust someone at school and there was less resistance getting him to school in the mornings.

Katie went on to explain that all parents of the class had received a letter from the headteacher informing them that Jack's class teacher had been suspended from immediate effect while investigations were taking place. The class teaching duties would be shared by two temporary teachers.

As Katie was telling me this her voice became higher pitched and her speech became louder and faster, the muscles in her face were pulled into a frown and her eyes were darting around. Katie said, "I've made a mess Luke, you know what I did? I rang the headteacher and yelled at him down the phone...how was Jack going to manage in a classroom with no warning of change and with two new members of staff, neither of whom would have an understanding of his needs. What do you think he thinks of me?" I looked at Katie, I thought about the situation in which she found herself; after years of difficulty with school, Jack was starting to have a better time of it, and much of this was down to the relationship with his new class teacher who, without warning, was now gone. So, I responded, "You know what I think, Katie? I think the headteacher thinks you are a loving mother who is worried about her son."

Katie looked me in the eye directly for the first time, exhaled deeply and said, "Do you think so Luke? I was thinking I could write a letter of apology and maybe ring back as well." I listened to Katie's plan to repair the situation with the headteacher and as we walked out of the school she said to me, "How come, Luke, I always feel calm when I'm with you?"

From an Emotion Coaching perspective, Luke's empathic response enabled Katie to feel safe and co-regulated. His empathy had helped activate her social engagement system and triggered the vagus nerve, helping her to feel calmer. Consider what might have happened if Luke had given any of the following responses:

- "OMG I can't believe that that's happened!"

  - Simply mirroring Katie's intense feelings may have just escalated the situation rather than calmed her.

- "What were you thinking, ringing and yelling at the head-teacher?!"

  - Reacting in a judgemental way may have escalated the situation and made Katie feel worse.

- "I'm sure it's not as bad as you think."

  - Minimizing and dismissing the situation may have made Katie feel ignored or unheard.

- "The same thing happened to me with my boss; you should have heard how he responded to me afterwards!"

  - Turning the conversation on to your own situation may make Katie feel insignificant.

Equally, a sympathetic response from Luke—"I'm sorry for you and for Jack"—may not have communicated to Katie that Luke understood her feelings. Katie was in a state of distress and a non-judgemental response, that stemmed from viewing the world as Katie saw it, helped to soothe and calm Katie's stressful feelings.

To summarize: be a STAR for the child

The 'STAR' acronym can be used as a reminder for what is involved in Step 1 of Emotion Coaching (Gus, 2018b).

STOP   Pause, don't react or speak straightaway. Notice any feelings the child's behavior may be bringing up in you.

THINK   What feeling might lay underneath the behavior I'm seeing? What is going on for the child right now?

ATTUNE   Attune to the feeling by putting yourself in the child's shoes.

REFLECT   What would be an equivalent situation for you that could cause you to feel that way?

Step 2: Labeling and validating a child's emotions

Labeling and validating feelings

With Step 1 about starting to feel and show empathy, Step 2 is about using language to reflect back to the child what they might be feeling and to validate those feelings. Phrases such as, "I think you may be feeling angry" or, "I wonder if you're worried" show the child that their emotions are real. This can be elaborated on by commenting, "I understand why you're cross about that" or, "I know you're disappointed and I'd feel the same," which validates the feelings. Using words to label the feeling allows you to validate and affirm the child's experience and emotions. This helps the child to feel seen and accepted and to learn that all feelings are normal, natural and okay. In this way, you are providing an essential narrative or translation of the emotional experience for the child. You are helping the child to make sense of their feelings, which helps them on their journey to self-regulation.

An example of how validating and labeling can help a child to feel calm comes from a secondary support teacher:

A 16-year-old boy returned to school after a long absence. I was concerned when he entered the support center as he was very hunched over and walked as though he were carrying a boulder on his back; his head hung down and he looked scared and exhausted. I thought he might be feeling wrung out with stress, overwhelmed and fearful. I suggested he took some time to settle into the room and into the space. I talked softly and slowly, as I felt he might be feeling over-stimulated. I maintained a very slow pace of speech and a calm tone of voice. I welcomed him back into school and gently gave him my observations of how he was presenting. I said, "You seem wrung out and tired."

The boy visibly relaxed. His body posture changed. He lifted his head and slowly began to make eye contact with me. He started to breathe more evenly and seemed to allow himself to become comfortable in the room. He began to talk about the discomfort he had been feeling in returning to school and to describe how all the lights and sounds were too much for him. He talked at length about the return to school and his experience of the lessons and the other children.

It is easier to attune, empathize, label and validate when there is only one pupil to deal with, but it is also possible in a busy classroom. Rob, a secondary school teacher, recounts how he empathized with, labeled and validated how a pupil new to his class might be feeling, which provided a positive basis for future interactions:

A 15-year-old student had recently started in my class, having moved schools. Senior leaders had advised not to push him too hard; however, I was concerned that he had spent a number of lessons either with his head in his hands or looking for distraction. I felt concern for his wellbeing and some anxiety that he wasn't engaging in tasks in lessons and was unsettling other students. I felt the student might be feeling some level of stress and confusion regarding the expectations of him and his expectations of himself. I approached him and said, "You seem stressed. I've noticed that your head's down and you're finding it difficult to get going." The student seemed a little surprised that he wasn't being reprimanded, but indicated that he didn't understand what he had to do. We talked about what he could do to let other people know that he was working. He agreed to show that he was working harder by concentrating on the task for an allocated time, which he succeeded in doing. The interaction improved the relationship that I had with the student and I was able to refer to it in subsequent lessons when he seemed reluctant to engage.

Labeling emotions

Labeling emotions appears to help connect the cognitive and emotional parts of the brain and can play a part in helping children to calm down. Matthew Lieberman's (2013) experimental work, measuring brain activity of people in MRI (magnetic resonance imaging) scanners, demonstrated that simply labeling the emotion that a person is experiencing reduced the intensity of brain activity associated with the emotion—labeling could be seen to be calming. Siegel (2012) calls this "name it to tame it." The following scenario shows how a primary headteacher used Emotion Coaching with a child who was angry:

A boy had been sent to my office and he was furious. He was huffing and puffing and kicking the wall. I went over to him, paused and then in a calm and gentle voice simply said, "I can see you're feeling really angry right now" and this literally took the wind out of his sails. He calmed down visibly before my eyes, he stopped kicking the wall and turned towards me. I couldn't believe it! I know it doesn't always work that way, but on this occasion it did, and we were able to sit together and talk calmly and rationally about the problem.

Simply asking a child to tell you what they are feeling in that moment may not be helpful. You may just get a shrug of the shoulder or a repeated vague answer such as "bored." This may not be because the child is trying to be difficult or defiant, but that they simply might not know the answer to the question "What are you feeling?" By noticing the child's verbal and non-verbal actions and responses to a situation, an attuned adult will be more likely to be able to interpret what it is they might be feeling and why. The labeling of the emotion lets the child know the adult is interested in them and that their feelings are real, so helping the child to make sense of what they are feeling and why. The following example shows how children learn from empathic experiences:

Jacob attended a specialist primary provision for children with social, emotional and mental health difficulties. Staff at his school had used Emotion Coaching as a style of communication with him since he started at the school two terms previously. Jacob had moved from being perplexed and sometimes resistant, to eventually accepting adults using an Emotion Coaching style with him. Subsequently, from a window in his classroom, Jacob saw his friend Harry outside furiously kicking the wall. Jacob opened the window and called out to him, "Harry kicking the wall won't make you feel better; go inside and talk to Sir, he'll tell you what you're feeling so you can start to feel better."

Attuned responses and labeling develop children's trust in adults and helps them to talk about their emotions. In doing so, and not being judged for feeling them, they feel safer and are more responsive to adult support. One boy said of his teacher who did Emotion Coaching with him, "He talks to me about what I am angry about and explains why I am angry and worried. Then I get on with my work, I get on with my day, because we have talked through my anger." Labeling a child's emotion gives the child a template for how to use language to express what they are feeling. Through modeling and scaffolding by the adult, children learn how to express their feelings through speech rather than behavior.

Benefits of describing what you see (non-verbal behaviors)

Sometimes just labeling the non-verbal behaviors that you see is a useful way to approach Step 2. It lets the child know that you have noticed them and are paying attention to how they feel. Sarah, a teacher, labeled seven-year-old Ruby's experience at the start of a reading task:

> Sarah asked Ruby if she could get her reading book to share with her in the reading corner of the classroom. Ruby was described as an anxious and quiet child with some learning needs. Ruby took a long time to get her reading book out of her bag and come to the reading corner. She sat fiddling with the book and Sarah wondered if Ruby was feeling worried about reading and maybe a bit embarrassed to say that she found it difficult. Sarah gently put her hand on Ruby's arm and said, "I noticed when you took the book out of your bag your face and body kind of changed from happy to sad."

Helen, a senior teacher, de-escalated a situation and helped move things forward by describing what she noticed about how Jay looked, and what he was doing:

> Helen was called into a classroom by a teacher and asked to remove Jay, who had hidden himself under a desk and was refusing to come out. Helen got down on the floor, so she was close to the table and said to Jay, "You're sitting under the table and curled up. I can see your face is looking cross." Because Helen demonstrated to Jay, without reprimand, that she could understand the distress he was experiencing, Jay started to feel seen and a little safer and connected to her. Helen went on, "It's not very comfortable or safe for you under the table. How about we go into my office, get a glass of water and find out what has gone on for you?" She reached out and gestured for him

to come to her. Jay moved slowly out from under the desk and went with Helen to her office.

Here are some examples of how to label and validate a child's emotions:

- "I can see that you get angry when that happens. I would feel angry if that happened to me. It's normal to feel like that."

- "I can see you're frowning and you're kicking the wall and you're expressing a lot of energy. If I didn't want to do something, I'd feel cross."

- "I've noticed you looking around at the others who are working on their projects. I wonder if you might be feeling nervous right now about whether your work will be okay. Have I got that right?"

Using the language of choice

While all emotions are natural and normal, they are not always a matter of choice. When speaking to children, adults can often say something like, "Was that behavior a good choice or a bad choice?" However, when we feel stressed or threatened, our stress response system is automatically activated and so for some children, there is no choice involved in their behavior. A child may have responded automatically, and logic, language and reasoning were not involved in the process—in other words, they did not make a conscious behavioral choice. Therefore, when children are repeatedly asked, "Was that a good choice or a bad choice?" they often can't give an answer and can then be deemed to be unresponsive or even truculent. Further, over time such a child may draw the conclusion that as an individual they must be "bad" as they are being told they're always making bad choices. One pupil in a school, after a steady diet of "good choice, bad choice" interrogations, cried, "Well, I think it must be me then, I must be bad."

For children who seem to have acted in a more premeditated manner, asking them to change their behavior, when they do not recognize or understand the underlying feeling which caused the behavior, is unlikely to lead to different behavior. Instead increasing disengagement and resentment build and the adult–child relationship, integral to the development of emotional competence in children, is not fostered.

Emotion labeling

For some people, labeling the emotions that a child may be experiencing can feel strange, particularly if that's not their usual way of communicating. Some worry that they might label the child's emotions incorrectly and some feel that it is "wrong" to tell a child how they are feeling. Moreover, a lack of confidence or experience can lead to some feeling that other people who are more skilled in dealing with emotions should be the ones to do the Emotion Coaching. But nothing is further from the case.

John Gottman's initial work on Emotion Coaching stemmed from observing families who were communicating and managing different emotions, including challenging ones. In other words, Emotion Coaching was not invented as a specialist therapy. It is just a natural and effective style of communication that some of us have always used, but we can all learn to use the style in a wider range of interactions with children. Indeed, the more Emotion Coaching is used with a child, the greater the opportunity for stimulating and strengthening neuronal pathways related to supporting emotional and behavioral self-regulation. Let's discuss further some of the concerns people have which can prevent them from labeling and validating children's emotions.

"It feels odd to label children's emotions"

Adults who are unaccustomed to using Emotion Coaching as a style of communication with children can sometimes feel that Step 2—labeling and validating emotions—feels odd and maybe even sounds mechanical. This is understandable as they are learning new skills. Think back to what we know about brain plasticity, growth and learning. When we first start to do something, it feels awkward, unnatural and forced. The brain connections involved in the action are not initially very strong. For example: when learning to drive a car, much thought has to go into coordinating the accelerator, brake and steering wheel, which initially may not be terribly successful or smooth. With practice and continuing to make the same sequence of actions, the brain pathways involved become stronger and faster. Finally, no thought is needed to change a gear, as it has become automatic. As one teacher puts it, "It can feel robotic in the beginning, but after a while you just incorporate it into your speech, and it starts to feel normal."

"I might label the emotions incorrectly"

A common reason for adults not using Emotion Coaching is the fear of "getting it wrong." "The child has been through so much already; I don't want to mess them up any further by making incorrect emotions–language connections!" said one teaching assistant.

If you are concerned about labeling a child's emotion incorrectly, please be reassured that it won't necessarily make it worse, and even if you get it wrong, you are still showing the child that you see them and are trying to connect with them. Even when you are trying very hard to attune to the child, you won't always get it right. Research about relationships by Tronick (1998) looked into what happens when there are "ruptures" (when an adult misattunes to the needs of a child) and "repair" (the reconnection between caregiver and child). Misattunement can involve many things, such as when a caregiver either isn't responsive to the child or doesn't reflect back appropriately what the child is feeling. Tronick found that misattunement is not the problem; indeed, we need to experience this as it is part of everyday life, but a lack of "reattunement" or "repair" is damaging. If there is no effort by the adult to reconnect with the child and make them feel seen and secure, the child suffers. Therefore, if you do get it a bit wrong, you can always try again because your attempt to continue to reach out, connect and understand the child is the key factor.

> *Megan was a mother and teacher who had consciously delayed using Emotion Coaching with her young daughter for many months after being introduced to the idea and the four-step framework. Megan was enthusiastic about the underpinning ideas and understood the value of Emotion Coaching, yet it took seven months before she used it with her preschool-aged daughter. This occasion turned out to be very successful and powerful. When questioned about why it had taken so long, Megan said simply, "I was scared of doing it wrong."*

"I might make it worse not better"

To explore this concern and offer some reassurance, we can look to the work of Winnicott (1953). He introduced the concept of "good enough parenting," which considered that being perfect caregivers all the time may not always be helpful. Indeed, if everything is perfect, children may not learn to adapt and develop skills to manage disappointments or adversity, and so develop resiliency. All this suggests that perceiving, interpreting and appropriately responding to a child's feelings does not always need to be done perfectly.

If you are feeling uncertain about which emotion to use in

labeling, a useful way forward is to use one of the five basic challenging emotions: anger, sadness, fear, disgust and surprise. One of these is likely to be at the core of what the child is feeling. If this does not help, you can always use a more generic term such as "upset," which might cover "sad,", "upset," "angry" or even "disappointed." However, because "upset" is a generic word for challenging emotions, we should avoid over-using it as this may prevent the development of more nuanced emotional literacy. Another way to mitigate the worry of "getting it wrong" is to begin your sentence with phrases like, "I wonder if you're feeling..." or being a little more tentative such as, "I'm thinking that maybe you're..." That being said, avoid being too vague as this might make the child feel that you are minimizing what they're feeling.

To help you with Step 2 here is a reminder of the five basic challenging emotions and some common secondary emotions that develop from them:

TABLE 3.1 EMOTION VOCABULARY

ANGER	SADNESS	FEAR	DISGUST	SURPRISE
Frustrated	Lonely	Worried	Disappointed	Confused
Mad	Hurt	Insecure	Bitter	Overwhelmed
Annoyed	Guilty	Embarrassed	Resentful	Startled
Offended	Uninterested	Rejected	Shameful	Shocked
Threatened	Inadequate	Vulnerable	Averse	Amazed

Word choice is especially important when we consider the age and developmental ability of the child. Therefore, you need to develop your own toolkit of phrases that you feel comfortable with, and that can be used appropriately and with sincerity, whatever the age of the other person.

"It's not okay to tell a child how they are feeling"

In child-centered learning which dominates much of Western culture, the emphasis is on the child being an active participant in their learning with the adult as facilitator. Because Emotion Coaching needs the adult to notice, empathize and then label and validate a child's emotions, it can be perceived as too adult driven. However, what the adult is actually doing here is allowing the child to co-opt their emotional regulation skills. The intention is to support the child to understand feelings; to help make the neural connections between the cognitive language, thinking part of our brain and the emotional feeling part of our brain. The aim is to scaffold the experience of emotional regulation.

In summary, your child's emotional development is unlikely to be impaired by less than perfect attempts at Emotion Coaching. Indeed, our research confirms a need to "practise to improve practice" as the more you consciously practice Emotion Coaching the easier and more natural it will become for you (Gilbert, 2018).

Pay attention to, and use Emotion Coaching with, lower levels of emotions

Gottman (Gottman and DeClaire, 1997) noted that parents who used Emotion Coaching with their children did so even when the children were displaying lower levels of emotions. They did not necessarily wait until the child had "flipped their lid" and was completely dysregulated. At school and at home, keep noticing and stay attuned to your children. For example, continue observing and watching the class even when it is quiet, and everyone is working on the task you had set. You will then be able to notice when a child starts to experience a change of emotion, and how this is displayed: the tapping of a pencil, swinging on a chair, staring out of a window. These are behaviors that might indicate low levels of more difficult emotions such as frustration, annoyance or disinterest. These can be noticed and dealt with empathically rather than being ignored or the adult waiting until disruptive behavior emerges.

The importance of Steps 1 and 2

Adults noticing and empathizing with a child's emotions, and then letting them know that they understand by labeling and validating them, enables the emotional brain to start to calm down, and this dampens our stress response system. This allows our brain to reconnect with the thinking brain and, when we feel safe again, use our social engagement system to drive our thoughts and actions. As Van der Kolk (2014, p.68 and p.62) noted:

> Sensing, naming and identifying what is going on is the first step to recovery... Being able to hover calmly and objectively over our thoughts, feelings and emotions...and then take our time to respond allows the executive [thinking] brain to inhibit, organize and moderate the hardwired autonomic reactions preprogrammed into the emotional brain.

With this in mind we will now look at Step 3.

Step 3: Setting limits

Emotion Coaching's Step 3 is the process of setting limits and in this section, we will explore some of the key issues. This is not just about ensuring that clear boundaries are set around unacceptable behavior, but also involves considering how to maintain the emotional regulation achieved in Steps 1 and 2 and your connection with the child. In particular, it is about avoiding re-igniting the child's distress as you attempt to impose limits on the child's behavior or desires. There are positive ways to communicate limit-setting, which maintain a child's sense of dignity and self-worth, may cause less distress and acknowledge the developmental nature of social, emotional and behavioral skills.

However, before we go any further there are two important caveats we should mention when thinking about Step 3. One, a child's safety is paramount and sometimes the need to stop the behavior overrides the need to use Emotion Coaching. Therefore, if a child is in danger or their actions risk the safety of others, the adult's role is to take immediate actions to ensure safety and protection. Emotion Coaching can then be used after the event to help the child make sense of the incident. Two, it is also important to note that sometimes Step 3 is not needed. This is true if the child's emotional turmoil has not led to inappropriate behavior. For example, if a child is sad because they have not been chosen for a sports team, and their behavior is appropriate, there is no need for limit-setting. Sadness is a normal emotional response to a denial of desire, and what they need is an empathic response and support to problem-solve how to manage their uncomfortable emotions.

When should limits be set?

Setting limits should only happen when the child has found an element of emotional calm. They need to be able to respond using rational thinking and cooperation, so using their social engagement system. This is the beginning of the co-learning phase of Emotion Coaching, in which you are not simply helping the child to become calm but are guiding them to learn and remember expectations.

Setting limits involves clearly stating the boundaries of acceptable behavior, preferably in a positive way. As this step includes ensuring that the child understands that some behaviors aren't acceptable, there can be a temptation to reassert behaviorist tendencies to do so. Some adults can misinterpret Step 3 as the point where they need to show and re-assert adult control and judgement. It then becomes a moment when their own emotions about the child's behavior may surface, for example saying, "Your behavior was terrible, and you have to control yourself" rather than the more positive approach, "Remember we all agreed that at school we use kind hands." If not careful, adults can inadvertently revert to a disapproving or authoritarian tone, which may lose the emotional connection made and lead to further dysregulation.

It is essential that limit-setting occurs when the child is able to listen, internalize and accept the boundary/rule without re-triggering a stress response. Therefore, the keys to success at Step 3 include ensuring that Steps 1 and 2 have enabled the child to experience effective co-regulation through empathy, labeling and validation, and maintaining this by carefully setting limits around the child's behavior, using positive language.

The role of the adult in setting limits: maintaining emotional regulation

What should be the aim of the adult at this point? Remember the power of emotional mirroring discussed in Chapter 1? Maintaining your role as a co-regulator is the foundation the child needs to enable them to experience boundaries in a way that is manageable and does not re-trigger overwhelming emotions. Emotion Coaching needs the adult to maintain their own emotional regulation and offer a sense of calm. This is important as it allows the child to see, feel and share the well-regulated adult brain, which supports their own regulation.

Maintaining co-regulation through this co-learning phase is vital. It is through effective limit-setting that we offer the child a safe space in which to acknowledge that it is the behavior that is not okay, while at the same time understanding that it is not them who is unacceptable. For this, the adult must consider how best to provide that safe space to maintain the child's dignity and emotional connection.

There are several factors that are particularly useful to consider at this point.

Thinking about body language and facial expression

You may recall from the first chapter how research indicates that a key feature of our brain's functioning is learning through social interactions (Lieberman, 2013). Indeed, Porges (2016) suggests that a large part of our ability to connect with others is dependent on understanding and using signals from faces and bodies. Remember that, unconsciously through neuroception and consciously through our learning experiences, we continually notice the words used and how the words are uttered—the speed and the pitch of the words, which words are emphasized and the use of pauses, non-verbals and gestures, facial expressions, head and hand movements and so on—to interpret and distinguish safety from danger. Also, our mirroring system is arguably one way our brains enable us to connect with the emotions of others (Cozolino, 2014). If someone smiles at you, notice how difficult it is for you not to smile back. It's the same with yawning...try it. Therefore, it's important to create and maintain effective interpersonal connectivity using your body and face.

Emotion Coaching helps you to establish and maintain respectful relationships with children. It provides social inter-actions that allow the child to feel safe—safe from shame and judgement about their emotions. It also shows the child that the adult wants to work with them to help them manage their behavior more effectively. Therefore, it is important to ask yourself, what is it that you wish the child to learn at this point? What are the important boundaries the child needs to understand and accept, and how can you use your voice, gestures and words to enable you to communicate in the most effective manner? Fatima recalls one particular lunchtime duty:

> *A ten-year-old pupil was sent out of the hall during lunchtime as he was displaying inappropriate behavior: growling and banging the table with his cutlery. I sat in front of the child and waited for him to stop banging. As soon as the banging subsided I verbally observed his behavior. "You seem very frustrated as you are banging and growling." When he hid his face and pushed his food away, I sat next to him and mirrored his body language and verbally observed it. "Now I am wondering if you are feeling sad because that is what I do when I am sad."*
>
> *The child told me that he was angry because he was told to use a knife and fork "properly" in front of his friends and he said he felt silly. I realized that he might also be feeling embarrassed and frustrated as he might be struggling to use his knife and fork, which he did not use often at home. I thanked him for telling me and said he could eat his dinner with me. I said that at school we eat our lunches with a knife and fork, and offered to show him by helping him cut up his food so he could continue to eat with a fork. The child allowed me to do this and so practiced how to follow the school's expectations.*

Fatima had paid attention to the child's body language, used her own body language to support calming (through mirroring) and used language to describe what she was seeing, as well as labeling and validating how the child might be feeling. Fatima then set limits on behavior by referring to school expectations. Expectations are different from rules as they are not clear cut. Expectations acknowledge that not all children may be able to meet desired standards of behavior at that particular point in time; they may need support or scaffolding to do so. Expectations rather than rules support the use of positive and constructive limit-setting. Some schools have substituted school and classroom "rules" for "expectations." This move acknowledges the role of the school in helping children develop social, emotional and behavioral skills rather than assume these are already in place.

Choosing words carefully: why word order can be important

As we mentioned earlier, it may initially feel awkward for some adults to affirm a child's feelings while also stating that certain behavior is not okay. How an adult chooses to phrase the limit-setting is important as some language can act as an incendiary device, re-triggering a defensive "flipped lid" response.

One common issue when setting limits is the word "but," which is often a default setting. For example, "I know that this feels uncomfortable for you and has made you frustrated, but hitting your sister is not okay." This sentence demonstrates empathy, and validation and labeling the emotions are also clear. However, the "but" may be heard by the child as a message that says, "how you feel actually isn't as important as what you've done!" The "but" may put the child back into a dysregulated state as it emphasizes the behavior rather than the emotion driving it:

> One teacher described a young girl, Abbi, who often "flipped her lid" when she did not get what she wanted. She became inconsolable and often had to be removed from the classroom, so was spending increasingly long times away from the class and her friends. Emotion Coaching was introduced and used by all the adults who worked with her, and they believed that Abbi became more responsive to them, noticeably calming down quicker. However, in Step 3, if they used the word "but" she reverted to her previous behavior and became inconsolable. They felt stuck and unable to help her to problem-solve and manage her strong emotions. Through trial and error, they learned to simply pause between affirming and empathizing with the feelings,

and then stating the school rules. Taking away the trigger word "but" worked and they felt that because Abbi was better able to calm down and remain calm, there was more opportunity to help her understand the school rules and so engage in the school community.

Consider the phrases used in limit-setting to positively build on the empathy shown in Steps 1 and 2. For example, rather than saying, "I know this feels uncomfortable and has made you frustrated, but you know the rules—no hitting in this house," you can set limits by stating the behaviors that are expected and acceptable, "I know this feels uncomfortable and has made you frustrated. When we play, we use safe hands in this house." However, if you feel you want to be more explicit about the need to stop the behavior quickly, you could just say "No hitting in our house" without the "but."

Alternatively, it may feel appropriate to use "but" as a way of distinguishing between the child's feelings and behavior. Our research shows that use of the word "but" does not always trigger dysregulation in children and can help the child to clearly understand what behavior is and isn't okay (Rose, Gilbert and McGuire-Snieckus, 2015). The key message here is, as always, about attunement with the child and trying different ways to express the limit-setting.

Another consideration is how adults' language can instil a sense of shame in a child. Even if it is unintentional, the tone and the words we use to describe a child's behavior may convey the message that it is the child themselves that is "naughty," "bad" or even "shameful." By the adult inadvertently passing judgement during the limit-setting phase, the behavior may be personalized to make it all about the child rather than their behavior. For example, the message here, "I know you're upset but you're being a bully and bullies are bad people" is that the child is believed to be a bully, therefore they are bad. These types of comments can lead to a sense of distress, loneliness and mistrust and fuel a negative evaluation of self.

Let's look at another example of limit-setting, where the adult successfully managed the first two steps but then inadvertently slipped into a more personal judgemental style of interaction during the limit-setting:

Matthew was a ten-year-old and had lost his temper in a lunchtime football game. He lashed out and kicked a friend, who went to the first aider to have his knee cleaned. Matthew had been sent inside and was visibly upset:

Teacher: Hi Matthew. I am so sorry to see that you're so upset. I heard that you haven't had a very happy lunchtime and that things got heated during the football game. I wonder if all that energy in the game got a bit too much and it meant that you got frustrated?

Matthew: They made me really mad.

Teacher: That sounds serious. I wonder what happened to make you so mad?

Matthew: They were running and running, and I couldn't keep up. Then Freddie kicked the ball and it hit me in the head really hard.

Teacher: Ouch! That must have hurt!

Matthew: Yeah, it did. And no one stopped to check if I was okay. So, when Freddie ran past me, I tripped him up and kicked him.

Teacher: That's a really difficult lunchtime isn't it? I know you and Freddie are usually such good friends, you must have felt really hurt and angry with him to kick him. But do you know what? In this school, we don't hurt other people, under any circumstances. And I am really disappointed that's the behavior you chose to use today, I thought more of you Matthew. You know that attacking other children isn't okay and you've really hurt Freddie.

Matthew: Well, I don't care what you think. He deserved it and more!

The teacher initially showed empathic labeling and validating of the emotions underlying Matthew's behavior, which was succeeding in connecting with Matthew and enabling the teacher to talk through the situation with him. However, when it came to the limit-setting (final paragraph) the teacher started to personalize her judgement by saying, "I thought more of you." She also reverted to "behavioral" thinking by making the assumption that Matthew had deliberately chosen to behave badly by saying "that's the behavior you chose to use today."

Although it can be argued that he did "choose" to trip up his friend, his actions were largely driven by his "downstairs" brain reacting to the physical attack—the hurt from the ball hitting his head, and the psychological attack—the injustice of no one stopping to see if he was okay. These incidents triggered a stress response, restricting access to and assistance from the thinking brain (prefrontal) and a reliance on behavior guided by the fight/flight mechanism. Therefore, his behavior did not reflect conscious reasoning and as a result was limited in scope and control.

The teacher's attempts at limit-setting changed the tone and nature of the connection, and the attunement, created through understanding the emotions underlying Matthew's behavior, ruptured and disappeared.

An alternative approach would be to specify or teach the behavior she would like to see in that scenario, which still incorporates and emphasizes limit-setting:

Teacher: That's a really difficult lunchtime isn't it? I know you and Freddie are usually such good friends, you must have felt really hurt

and angry with him to kick him. In school, we play safely with each
other. Remember what we all agreed to do, when we're upset—we
step out of the game for a little while. This helps us all to stop and
calm down.

This version states the behavior that is desirable and retains Matthew's dignity. It also makes the expectations clear. This language is inclusive and unprejudiced, reinforcing what is expected and reminding Matthew of things he should and could do to help regulate his feelings and play safely.

Separating the adult's emotion from that of the child: putting on your own oxygen mask before attending to the child's

Practitioners have been known to say that despite their use of Steps 1 and 2, and their careful use of Step 3, Emotion Coaching still doesn't seem to work. It is important to accept that Emotion Coaching is not a panacea that will work every time, with every child.

One problem that may arise is when adults are unaware, ignore or find it hard to manage their own emotional world and keep their agenda outside the process of Emotion Coaching a child. We all have emotions, and we know they are designed to make it difficult to ignore them. Our own feelings can be strong and intrude and can effectively derail the process. It is particularly easy for this to happen in Step 3, when we can revert to behaviors based on impulse and habit and rely on our physical strength and power to achieve a satisfactory outcome for the adult.

Consider the example of three-year-old Zoey with her childminder, Sue. Sue was picking her up from nursery, but Zoey wanted to continue playing with her chosen toy:

Sue: I know you want to carry on playing rather than going home today. I can see that it looks really colourful and fun to play with.

Zoey: I don't want to go home!

Sue: Come on and leave it now. We've got to get home on time tonight.

Zoey: No!

Sue: Do you know what? I don't have time for this messing about. You've played with these toys all day and now you need to leave them and come on, so. (Picks up the child)

Zoey: (Crying and struggling) I don't want to!

In this situation, Sue feels under the pressure of time. She needs Zoey to stop playing and come with her to get home. Again, this situation started off well with Sue recognizing, labeling and validating the child's emotions. But the interaction derailed at limit-setting and Sue reverted to her agenda and used physical power to achieve her goal, rather than help Zoey understand why they needed to leave. Thinking ahead, and perhaps using the STAR acronym (Gus, 2018b) mentioned in Step 1, may have helped Sue to remain calm and achieve the desired outcome, while helping Zoey learn about rules and routines.

Then Sue might say:

Sue: I know you want to carry on playing rather than going home today. I can see that it looks really colourful and fun to play with.

Zoey: I don't want to go home!

Sue: I understand you're upset. You want to keep playing.

Zoey: Yes.

Sue: I know it's hard to stop when you're having fun.

Zoey: Why can't I stay?

Sue: It would be nice to stay, I know. Hey, it's getting dark outside now, so the nursery has to close. Look, everyone's putting on their coats and going home for their tea. I'm feeling hungry too, are you? And I'm making sausages tonight. Let's go ask Hayley [Zoey's key person] if we can put this toy in a special place for you so you can play with it again tomorrow.

The benefits of consistency in approaches within the school or home

In a school setting, there are many different adults with whom a child interacts. The benefits of a whole-school approach, where all the staff use Emotion Coaching can be seen in the following example.

As you may recall, in Step 2, we met Maria who was supporting Sam in his science lesson and, when he "flipped his lid," Maria used Emotion Coaching to help Sam manage his emotions. He eventually became visibly calmer. She had felt that he was now able to talk and listen using his thinking brain, and they were ready to discuss different ways Sam could manage his emotions for more constructive outcomes. However, the arrival of a different adult, who decided to impose limits on behavior using a more traditional behavioral perspective, caused Sam to become dysregulated again.

A senior teacher came out into the corridor and saw what was going on between Maria and Sam. She saw the scattered wheelchairs and knocked over walking frames and in a very angry tone of voice said, "Sam I'm really sad that you did all of this. All these children need their equipment; how would you like it if they came and broke your things. You know what will happen for such naughty behavior and I hope you're going to pick it all up and apologise."

Sam stared at the ground, his face became red. Maria felt that Sam was experiencing shame and fear, and this was communicated by petulant and angry behavior. Maria explained that she and Sam were in the process of clearing up and the teacher went back to her room.

Maria and Sam returned to the chill-out zone as Sam looked as if he was about to erupt again, so Maria began Emotion Coaching all over again...

Although this is a complex example, it does reveal a lot about how positive limit-setting in Step 3 reinforces and builds on the work of Steps 1 and 2. It also reveals the need for consistency in the approaches of all adults working with children, and how inconsistency hinders not helps children to develop and manage self-regulation. Let's now take a look at the final step.

Step 4: Problem-solving

Problem-solving is the final part of the Emotion Coaching process and gives the child an opportunity to work with you to explore and understand their responses to emotions. It includes discussions about what happened during the emotional moment, helping the child build a narrative of the event. These narratives contribute to a child's internal working model which guides their understanding about relationships and informs subsequent behaviors. The narratives will also influence their emerging meta-emotion philosophy—their reactions and responses and reasoning to emotions in themselves and others. Problem-solving, scaffolded by adults, assists children to learn about emotions and self-regulation. They can develop skills or tools for their toolkit for life, allowing them to engage in a greater variety of situations and to manage the ups and downs of everyday living. In this section, we will discuss the purpose of problem-solving and how Step 4 empowers children to take increasing ownership of their emotions and behaviors and contributes to the skills of resiliency. We will also explore the interplay between Step 3, setting limits, and Step 4.

The purpose of problem-solving

When Step 4 has been reached, the child is ready and more able to talk about what happened, why it happened and, most importantly, how they could have handled things differently. At this point, the adult offers developmentally appropriate support, recognizing that feelings and emotions may at times be beyond our control, but that how we react and behave in response to them—our behavior—can be managed. With practice, how we behave can become a matter of choice, even when experiencing difficult emotions.

Step 4 teaches children that through self-control, conflicts can be managed and resolved peacefully. An ability to delay gratification and demonstrate self-control is positively linked with academic outcomes; the more a person is able to resist impulses, the more likely they are to be academically successful (Duckworth and Seligman 2005). Indeed, Lieberman (2013) proposes that self-control is like a muscle, in that practice makes it stronger. John Gottman and DeClaire (1997) suggest that just as children with good muscle tone and strength do well in sporting activities, children with good vagal tone are better at responding to and recovering from emotional stress. Therefore, adults who use Emotion Coaching provide children with many opportunities to be co-regulated, to practice their skills and develop repertoires to self-regulate. By copying and experiencing attuned adult responses and practicing self-regulation, children can develop and improve their own vagal tone.

The process of problem-solving requires a child to consider how to engage their capacity for self-control and adapt previous behavioral responses to be more advantageous and in line with social expectations. Success justifies and reinforces change and the newly acquired self-regulatory skills can then be applied to other areas of a child's learning—a process that could lead to better academic performance (Gus *et al.*, 2017; Rose *et al.*, 2019). We suggest that actively engaging in problem-solving offers benefits that potentially have an impact on a child's brain development.

Emotion Coaching requires an ongoing interpersonal connection, which in this problem-solving step allows the adult to guide the child to consider different versions of the future. Step 4 offers children a relationship that accepts (because we all make them) unavoidable and predictable mistakes in behavior made as a consequence of emotions. It provides an opportunity for learning about themselves, the world around them and their own impact on others within it.

For example: Dylan and Ritchie were five years old and had fought over who was to be the driver of the car they had made together in the playground. Dylan had pushed Ritchie hard out of the front seat, and he had fallen and hurt his arm. Both boys were upset, and Ritchie went off with the lunchtime supervisor to have his arm cleaned. Jamal, their teacher, used Emotion Coaching to help Dylan calm down and they talked about the importance of using "kind hands" and "following school expectations" when sharing toys and equipment. He now felt that Dylan was ready to problem-solve:

Jamal: Your friend got in the driver's seat first. I'm wondering if that made you feel really angry because you wanted to be first in the car you'd made?

Dylan (looks up): Yes, it's not fair. I made the car. It's mine, not his.

Jamal: So you felt that because you'd built most of the car it was your right to be the driver and not his?

Dylan: Yes.

Jamal: And now Ritchie is upset and has a sore arm (pause). Pushing other people is dangerous because people get hurt. Can you think of another way you could have let Ritchie know you were unhappy?

Dylan: Well, I could say...Ritchie, this is my car and I am the driver?

Jamal: Great start. I'm wondering if Ritchie perhaps thought it was both your car as he built it too?

Dylan (nodding): Well, he could have sat next to me?

Jamal: Good idea, Dylan. Ritchie could have sat next to you on your adventure. Perhaps you could take it in turns so he got a turn to be driver too?

Dylan: Hmmm...yeah, maybe.

Jamal: I'm wondering where Ritchie is now? He seemed to be really shocked. He wasn't expecting to be pushed. Shall we go and find him?

Dylan: I'm not saying sorry....

Jamal: So, you don't feel like apologizing right now. But shall we just go and check that he's okay?

Dylan: Okay.

When Jamal and Dylan arrive back at the car, Ritchie has a plaster on his arm and is sitting in the car. Without prompting, Dylan says, "Alright, Ritchie? Sorry I pushed you. I know, let's drive together and take turns to be the big driver."

Through this interaction, Jamal was encouraging Dylan to understand how Ritchie might have felt as a result of his actions, and to consider a different version of the future. Jamal genuinely listened to Dylan and his views and encouraged him to think about how to solve the problem in a more acceptable way. This example shows how Jamal guided Dylan through the process of problem-solving to come up with a solution that was acceptable and appropriate. It also permitted Dylan to feel that he was able to have agency within his world and practice taking responsibility.

Ownership and empowerment: solutions for the future

When we experience overwhelming emotions that result in challenging or unacceptable behavior, the chance to consider what happened and why can help a child understand. This then enhances their ability to reflect on their behavior and its impact on others, developing perspective-taking skills and contributing to their ability to repair and restore relationships. Step 4 is the opportunity to discuss what happened and to consider other behaviors for the next time the child experiences those strong emotions. The key question is therefore, "What would you do next time you feel like that?"

The child has co-regulated thanks to Steps 1 and 2 and is clear about the limits around expected behaviors (Step 3). By asking the child to consider other possible ways of behaving, the adult is offering choice. The message that all emotions are acceptable is maintained, while also acknowledging that perhaps things could have been handled differently, and considering what might "differently" look like for the child?

An eight-year-old girl had a loud tantrum in her classroom during a literacy lesson. Her teacher completed Steps 1, 2 and 3 with her and then started problem-solving:

Teacher: So, when you feel really frustrated because the writing is too hard, I know that all your frustration pops out suddenly and you feel you can't help getting upset.

Chloe: I can't help it.

Teacher: I know that it feels like that. I know that this written work is something you find tricky and I want to help as soon as you are beginning to feel a bit wobbly or unsure. I wonder whether there is anything you could do next time you feel like that to let me know?

Chloe: I don't know.

Teacher: Well, let's have a think. See if you could come up with something you could do to let me know when things aren't going right. Could you do that for me?

Chloe: Okay.

It is important to note that the child in this scenario is being given time to think about what she would like to do instead—her teacher is not giving her solutions. As adults, thanks to being older and more experienced, we have much knowledge and many ways of deciding how to behave. As a result, it can be tempting to offer up our own strategies for the child to implement, particularly when time is short. However, by allowing the child to develop their own ideas around alternative responses to emotions, we are teaching them that, first, their behavior can be a personal choice and that, second, they have the resources within themselves to both manage and change their behavior.

Important learning comes from the discussions about their own resolutions that help to strengthen a child's capabilities and resilience. This kind of conversation, regarding the child's own resolutions, allows the development of autonomy in managing their own feelings and behavior choices.

However, this opportunity can be challenging and may initially need adult support. It should be remembered that, as Gottman and colleagues (1997) suggest, for younger or less able children, adults' ideas are invaluable as their ability to think of solutions may be limited. The message therefore is to work together to find a solution using the child's own ideas whenever possible. The adult might need to scaffold the problem-solving with additional suggestions about what they can practically do, rather than offering strategies to help the child calm down. A key part of Step 4 remains an ongoing attuning to the child and their ability to suggest solutions.

Problem-solving frameworks

Step 4 of Emotion Coaching can incorporate a variety of problem-solving methods (see Chapter 6 for supporting complementary strategies). Which one to use is determined by your relationship with the child, their developmental level and the time available.

A simple model is to think about how you can help the child:

- Explore the child's feelings and needs that gave rise to the problem. Maybe help the child to think about what they were trying to achieve with their behavior, what they wanted to stop or get started: "What were you wanting to happen?" "What were you trying to achieve by...?"

- Increase awareness of emotions by asking how the emotions made the child feel: "How were you feeling when that happened?" "What did it make you feel like?" "Have you felt that way before?"

- Share ideas to identify more constructive ways of expressing their feelings through other behavior. This might be achieved through scaffolding their thinking: "Let's think of what you could have done instead of hitting out," "We can make a list together of ideas," "If I help you, we can decide what is best," "Can you think of a different way to deal with your feelings?" "I can help you to think of a different way to cope," "Can you remember feeling this way before and what you did?" "Have you thought about doing this instead?"

- Agree a solution so that the child has alternative options for next time: "Let's decide what you can do next time you feel like this," "When you feel like this again you can try..." "Try and do this next time you feel like this," "Let's decide what you will do next time you feel like this," "Do you think doing that would be more helpful for you and others?"

Problem-solving does not need to be complicated or time consuming. Once you've carried out Steps 1 and 2, sometimes it is just a reminder of a previous discussion. Danni, a teaching assistant, recalls when Muhammad, an eight-year-old boy who found literacy difficult, refused to do work in class. He folded his arms and then stormed off to the cloakroom.

I followed Muhammad into the cloakroom and after waiting a few minutes to give him a chance to calm down, I approached him, got down to his level and sat with him. I said to Muhammad that he looked really sad and a bit cross and checked with him that this was correct. I then went on to wonder that maybe he felt this way because the work looked hard and he was worried about not being able to do it. Muhammad agreed and added that he would "look dumb" if he got it wrong. I tried to convey empathy with my facial expression and body movements and went on to add that I too found it hard when I had to learn new things.

As neutrally as possible, limits were then set. Muhammad was gently reminded that we had talked before about how everyone in school has to at least try to do the work. I reminded him that we had talked about the things he could do when he was feeling like this, instead of going to the cloakroom. He said he had forgotten so we talked about them again and about the ways he could let me know when he was feeling like this. I reassured him of what I could do to help him with his work. Muhammad said writing down what to do next time would help him remember and we agreed to meet again to see how things were going.

Danni reported that Muhammad relaxed as soon as she reflected his feelings back to him. Being calmer, he was able to remember and share the different ways to try to manage strong emotions and let Danni know when he was struggling. She reassured him of her support and Muhammad was able return to the classroom and get on with the set task a few minutes later. In this short interaction, Muhammad had experienced an attuned adult demonstrating that she understood and empathized with the strong feelings that he was finding difficult to manage. Danni's support allowed him to express his feelings as well as reminding him of the class expectations. Her response empowered him to take ownership of his feelings and reassured him that he could find ways to manage in the future. In this example, the problem-solving was straightforward. While Danni could have taken a behavioral approach, there would then have been little learning about emotions and development of skills to help him manage.

The interplay between setting limits and problem-solving

There are scenarios in which setting limits and problem-solving may need to be placed in a different order, with problem-solving (Step 4) coming before limit-setting (Step 3). This is particularly so if Emotion Coaching is being used with an adult who is experiencing dysregulated emotions.

Mandy, a parent, came into the classroom at the end of the day. She was very angry because the teacher, Paul, gave her son a sanction that they thought was unfair. Mandy had not arranged an appointment and so had taken Paul by surprise. However, he tried to use Emotion Coaching to diffuse the situation. It seemed to be going well until Step 3, setting limits:

Mandy: I'm here because I'd like to know why you think the punishment you gave Connor yesterday is fair?

Paul: Hello, Mrs Winters. I wonder whether you have a bit of time to sit with me and chat about this? I know that it seems as if what I've done is unfair and that's frustrating.

Mandy: Yes, it is. Because he's come home really upset and I'm not having it.

Paul: It's horrible when they come out of school and they're upset, and I am really sorry that's happened.

Mandy: Yeah, it is.

Paul: I also want to mention that you should really have made an appointment to see me. If one parent decides they can come in at any time, all parents can start doing that and it makes things so difficult. That's why we have an appointment system.

Mandy: Do you want to know something, I don't care about the school system; I just want to know what happened to Connor and why you upset him!

In this situation, the limit-setting (final paragraph) negated the calming effect of Steps 1 and 2. Paul felt deflated and unable to engage Mandy, who was now angrier than she was when she arrived, in any problem-solving. Here is another version of this conversation, and this time Step 3 comes at the end of the interaction:

Mandy: I'm here because I'd like to know why you think the punishment you gave Connor yesterday is fair?

Paul: Hello Mrs Winters. I wonder whether you have a bit of time to sit with me and chat about this? I know that it seems as if what I've done is unfair and that's frustrating.

Mandy: Yes, it is. Because he's come home really upset and I'm not having it.

Paul: It's horrible when they come out of school and they're upset, and I am really sorry that's happened.

Mandy: Yeah, it is.

Paul: Here, take a seat. This is what happened [teacher explains]. So his behavior was a bit of a problem and I am really pleased to be able to talk to you about it. Do you think we can put our heads together and work out what's going on for Connor at the moment and see if we can work together to come up with an action plan to help support him in the right way?

Mandy: Yes, that sounds helpful.

Mandy and Paul decide a plan of action to support Connor.

In this scenario, rather than limit-setting and then problem-solving, the parent is being included in the problem-solving and tackling the key source of Mandy's stress. This approach has created an opportunity for the teacher to work with the parent and develop a more trusting, open and supportive line of communication. Mandy now understands why her son was disciplined, and so can find a resolution to her initial concern, and a shared plan of action. It is now possible to set limits. For example, at the end of the discussion, the teacher might say:

Paul: Thanks so much, this has been such a useful discussion and I'm really glad we have a way forward that we are both happy with. It would actually be really useful if we could do this again, so if there's ever another time when you feel as if you need a word with me, I wonder if you wouldn't mind calling the office and letting them know that you're coming in? It makes it a lot easier for me to make sure I'm not busy with someone else, and I can give you my full attention.

However, it is always important to remember that although Steps 3 and 4 may be, or need to be, interchangeable, this can only occur if Steps 1 and 2 are firmly in place. The first two steps allow successful co-regulation to occur and without this, Steps 3 and 4 are likely to be less successful.

A reminder of the four-step Emotion Coaching framework

This chapter has looked in detail at how you might "do" Emotion Coaching. Adults using Emotion Coaching in educational and community settings report finding the four-step framework helpful during busy periods and that it gives them the confidence to manage situations. Table 3.2 recaps the four-step framework and summarizes the adult's role at each step.

TABLE 3.2 FOUR-STEP FRAMEWORK OF EMOTION COACHING (© EMOTION COACHING UK)

	Four-steps of Emotion Coaching	What the adult can do
STEP 1	Recognize the child's feelings and empathize with them	Stop, Think, Attune, Reflect
STEP 2	Label the feelings and validate them	Use emotional words and supportive gestures
STEP 3	Set limits on behavior if needed	Let the child know what is expected
STEP 4	Problem-solve with the child	Problem solve "with" not "for" the child

Chapter 4

Using Emotion Coaching Effectively

When we use Emotion Coaching, it is likely to be influenced by our own reactions to and reasoning about children in distress or who are exhibiting challenging behavior. Our approach will reflect an awareness of emotions in ourselves and in others, while our style is influenced by the repertoire of "tools" we have to manage behaviors and perceived desired outcomes. In this chapter, we will take a closer look at the relationships between our emotional reactions, responses and reasoning and how we use them to support our Emotion Coaching practice.

It's tempting to just list when and when not to use Emotion Coaching but that would be neither simple nor helpful. Although we can assure you of what Emotion Coaching is not, we can only be tentative when recommending when Emotion Coaching may or may not be appropriate. This is because Emotion Coaching relies heavily on your own perceptions and assessment of the child's needs in that moment. It will be you who decides when to use Emotion Coaching and with whom, how long to spend on each step, when to move between the steps, and the order of the steps.

Only you can take into consideration the context and situation, your relationship with the child, and their developmental abilities, and only you know your rationale and the time available to do Emotion Coaching.

Therefore, in this chapter, we draw attention to and ask you to reflect on what the adult contributes to Emotion Coaching. From our research with practitioners and parents, we share the most frequent considerations and caveats for Emotion Coaching practice, and hope, in this way, to empower you to decide when to use this approach.

What we feel about feelings and behavior

Our responses to feelings and behavior reveal a range of underlying thoughts and feelings such as:

- our ability to manage our own feelings generated by the child's feelings and behavior

- our values and beliefs about how feelings should be expressed

- our underlying values and beliefs about behavior and how it should be managed.

These will be influenced by:

- how we feel about emotional behaviors and displays in ourselves and others

- how much we trust or believe in our own feelings

- how we regulate our own feelings

- how effective we are at managing our emotions.

Meta-emotion philosophy

John Gottman and his colleagues coined the phrase meta-emotion to explain emotional feelings and behaviors (Gottman *et al.*, 1997). Meta-emotion refers to knowledge of reactions, responses and reasoning about emotions in oneself and others. There are recognizable types of meta-emotion, which can be categorized as dismissing, disapproving, laissez-faire and Emotion Coaching (Gottman *et al.*, 1997). However, everyone's meta-emotion is unique, and is known as your meta-emotion philosophy. A person's meta-emotion philosophy is complex and nuanced and changes over time and through experience. Although we often are unaware of our meta-emotion philosophy, it is initially shaped by early encounters with emotions in a person's family of origin and with significant others.

From our childhood experiences, we also build "internal working models," which provide us with a mental representation or event scripts about the self and others. The idea of internal working models is drawn from attachment theory (Bowlby, 1988). Continuing research in attachment theory suggests that a caregiver's responses to a baby's stress, whether this is driven by purely physical needs such as hunger or a psychological need such as the need to feel loved, directly affect how the baby learns to cope with the stress of life.

Internal working models allow us to predict, control and manipulate our environments, interpret our own and others' actions and behaviors, and so guide our interaction with others. It is therefore fair to assume that our meta-emotion philosophy and internal working models are closely aligned and are influenced by one another. Both Sroufe (1995) and Fonagy and colleagues (2004) have suggested that the internal working model is foundational to a child's future relationships and mental health—no wonder that early childhood experiences are thought to be significant in shaping who we become.

It stands to reason that an infant who receives consistent, responsive and attuned nurturing from their caregivers is more likely to categorize their day-to-day interactions and experiences to create a positively biased internal working model of memories. Their meta-emotion philosophy is also more likely to reflect and replicate empathic reactions, responses and reasoning to emotions and emotional behaviors. Indeed, long-term studies have shown that children with responsive caregivers generally have higher self-esteem, better emotional self-regulation and more resilience (Sroufe and Siegel, 2011). Conversely, the child that receives inconsistent, misattuned or detrimental care and attention in their everyday interactions is more likely to operate with a negative bias to future interactions. Their meta-emotion philosophy may lead them to be suspicious and mistrusting of emotions in themselves and others and to lack confidence in how to interpret and respond to emotional displays.

Havighurst and colleagues (2009) have highlighted how Emotion Coaching can contribute to children's internal working models through the adult guiding children's thoughts, feelings and behavior, thereby making an explicit link to attachment theory. By using emotion-focused talk, essentially a dialogue, which enables children to feel appreciated and soothed, adults can teach children to use appropriate strategies to cope with stress. Children feel able to explore feelings and relationships by reflecting with others. This allows them to confront their anger, fear and anxiety safely, rather than projecting them through challenging behavior. Emotion Coaching assists children to develop an internal dialogue about social and emotional experiences, developing their meta-emotion philosophy to support them in regulating their behavior.

Raising emotional awareness

Raising awareness of your own reactions, responses and reasoning about emotions is key in developing your use of Emotion Coaching. Awareness of our meta-emotion philosophy can give the insight and greater confidence needed to support children who may be experiencing strong emotions that alone they are unable to manage (Rose, Gilbert and McGuire-Snieckus, 2015; Gilbert, 2018; Gus, 2018a).

For example, Chris, now an experienced assistant headteacher, recalls a formative incident in his first year of teaching, when a pupil rejected his attempts to comfort him. He describes how this incident was critical in raising his awareness of the power of emotions and the importance of building real connections with all children:

We had a boy called Daryl in our school who was known for having difficulties with his behavior, so it wasn't unusual for me as his form teacher to be talking to him and reminding him about appropriate actions or words. I remember packing up at the end of the day and the children were lining up to leave the room. An incident happened and Daryl fell as the children left the room. My first instinct was to raise my voice at him and say, "See I told you that was going to happen if you behaved like that," but then I realized he was embarrassed and actually hurt, so I went closer to him and said, "Are you okay? Come on, get up," but Daryl had a further meltdown, yelling at me, "Just go away! You don't care anyway."

I felt shocked as this was the exact opposite. I did care—I cared a lot about all the children in the class. Daryl got up and without looking at me left the room, and I didn't go after him to check he was really okay. I was left alone in the classroom feeling misunderstood, rejected and hurt. I felt I had failed him and myself as a teacher.

As I watched Daryl walk across the playground to go home,

I reflected on how unpleasant it was for me, as an adult to experience these feelings, and wondered whether Daryl may feel like this—rejected and ignored by me. Our relationship was neither mutual nor nurturing but driven by my desire, as a new teacher, to do whatever I needed to ensure Daryl made the most of his learning and everyone remained safe. However, here was the evidence that I did not make him feel seen or safe and our relationship did not let him trust me to calm him when he was distressed. I realized I had created more not fewer difficulties for myself and for Daryl and his learning.

How the incident had made me feel mattered—it made me aware of the power of emotions and how they informed behaviors. It exposed the necessity to show—as an adult—that I cared about them all as individuals. I needed relationships that were empathic if I wanted to be a better teacher. Daryl was a boy who shaped the teacher I am today.

As Chris found out, we have to accept, whether we like it or not, that we all have emotions, and most are supposed to make us feel uncomfortable enough to do something different.

Thinking about your meta-emotion philosophy

When it comes to exploring your meta-emotion philosophy, you must first carve out time for yourself. It is important that you are interested, but you need to have compassion for yourself in this process. It's about being curious rather than critical, and open-minded rather than judgemental.

To start to explore your meta-emotion philosophy, reflect on your emotions in the home and at work as well as in your personal and professional lives. Think about these areas:

- How were emotions displayed and received when you were a child. Were some emotions more acceptable than others?

- What were your experiences, and what were your take-away messages about emotions?

- Was anger tolerated or punished? Did your parents try and distract you from your sadness or share your joy with you?

- Do you respond in the same way to emotions at home as you do to emotions at work?

By identifying some of the emotional messages you received from your own parents, siblings, extended family, friends and carers, you can start to build a sense of how you feel about emotions. By considering how you respond to them and how you explain, or justify, them in yourself and others, you'll raise your awareness and discover more about your meta-emotion philosophy. You can then use this insight to help you imagine how others might be feeling and to shape a response informed with genuine empathy. Reflecting on feelings and naming them, and then responding to what others need in the moment, can help to reduce the impact of our own, often unconscious, meta-emotion philosophy. It's essentially a case of "putting on the oxygen mask first" before helping the child.

Here's another way to explore your meta-emotion philosophy and to think about what you do to self-regulate and what helps you calm yourself down. Either use the example below or, if you prefer, think about a recent incident when you experienced strong or difficult emotions, such as anger, shock, frustration, embarrassment, sadness...or a combination of them all.

Example: You see a child having a tantrum in the middle of the playground because their childminder refuses to let them stay to play after school?

Keeping the scenario or your own incident in mind, ask yourself:

- How does it make you feel? What words would you use to

describe the feelings (e.g. angry, shocked, frustrated, embarrassed, amused, horrified, impatient, irritated, sad, tired or a combination of these words)?

- What actually happens in your body and where do you feel the feelings?

- How do you feel about what's happening to you? Do the feelings make you then feel uncomfortable, empowered, scared, guilty, energized, embarrassed, alive?

- Does the incident take you back to when you were a child, remembering how you were treated and how that made you feel?

- Does the feeling and watching emotional displays cause alarm bells to ring and make you feel uncomfortable?

It's worth remembering that we cannot co-regulate if we don't know how to self-regulate. Knowing about your emotional self, what situations make you "flip your lid," how that feels, what happens, and what helps you to feel calmer will give you a better understanding of your meta-emotion philosophy and how emotions inform behavior. How you respond and your awareness of when you feel sad, angry or frightened affects how you respond to a child who is sad, angry or frightened.

The following example shows how a practitioner was able to develop a working relationship with a parent once she had recognized that her meta-emotion philosophy was interfering with achieving an empathic connection:

Jen was a successful pastoral lead in a large school. She was concerned about a child, Alice, who was struggling academically and becoming increasingly disruptive. Although Jen phoned Alice's dad weekly, she had never managed to get him to come to the school to talk things over. Indeed, she had begun to dread phoning because the conversation quickly became confrontational when she tried to explain their concerns about his daughter. The calls always ended either with the dad shouting at her that the school did not really care and slamming the phone down or Jen becoming so angry and frustrated at his rudeness and inability to listen that she would tell him so and terminate the call.

After training in Emotion Coaching, Jen spent some time thinking about her own meta-emotion philosophy and what, perhaps, she herself brought to the telephone conversations. She knew that rules and respect were very important to her, and she had always found that they helped to maintain control and contain emotions. She prided herself on not having to think about emotions much and being indifferent to emotional displays. She wondered about the effects of having grown up on a military base where respect was directly linked to status. Rarely were strong emotions seen or expressed and if they were, they were dealt with quickly, using behaviorist tactics. She realized that on the rare occasions that she was challenged, she felt this as a personal attack and often used her status to shut it down and regain power. This realization led her to reflect on her conversations with Alice's dad, and whether her approach—her choice of words and the tone she used in response to the rudeness—was inflaming rather than controlling the situation.

As a result, she decided to try to use Emotion Coaching when she next phoned Alice's dad. When he started to accuse the school of "always picking on Alice, never giving her a chance," Jen did not immediately try to defend the school's action. Jen recognized the strong emotions informing the dad's behavior and decided to manage her response to make a connection that calmed rather than exacerbated. She responded by pausing, checking how she was feeling, and then said that she could "hear that he was really angry" and that "she'd be upset too if she thought the school was picking on her daughter." The dad stopped shouting, paused and in a more controlled, quieter tone said, "Too right I'm angry." Jen assured him that she understood and "got" how angry he was. When he had audibly calmed, she said she was sorry that he thought that the school was picking on the family, that there were crossed wires here, that the school, like the dad, wanted only to help Alice. She was able to explain the reason for the calls, that the school very much wanted and needed his support to find the best way to do this for Alice. The dad listened to what Jen had to say and, as a result, agreed to visit the school and to work together on a plan to help Alice get back on track.

In a subsequent meeting, Jen told the dad of her earlier fears of phoning him; he was surprised and embarrassed, and having been unaware of his intimidation, he apologized. He explained that he had felt overwhelmed by the apparent injustice, believing that the school just wanted to get rid of Alice. However, as a result of the recent contact with Jen, he felt that he could trust the school to care about his daughter's future. Jen felt that, before training in Emotion Coaching, it had not occurred to her how important it was to be aware of her own emotions and how much she could contribute and influence the outcome of such an encounter.

How do you manage your emotions?

Although we have many ways to manage emotions, people are individuals so there is no one strategy that works for all. We have to learn which are the most effective ways through trial and error, copying and repetition.

Take a moment to think about what strategies you use—the tools in your toolkit—that help you to manage different intensities of emotions, calm yourself, and self-regulate. Do you distract yourself by doodling, staring out of the window or start to count things in your head, or do you physically move away from the source of stress and focus on your breathing to help regulate and keep it steady, tighten and relax your fists or tap your foot? Do you go for a run, chill with friends, have a soak in the bath, play music, do a jigsaw puzzle, go for a walk, eat or drink something comforting? What about when you're at work, what do you do there to manage your emotions?

Think about what the mental signs and bodily sensations are that show you are calming down, and how calming down feels. By raising your awareness of how emotions make you feel, how you react and what you do to self-regulate you are able to practice attuning to emotions, which in turn helps you to attune to and support others. Time spent exploring your meta-emotion philosophy will add to your skills in Emotion Coaching. Knowledge and understanding of calming strategies can be used to support Steps 1, 2 and 3 and to scaffold the problem-solving stage of Emotion Coaching.

Using Emotion Coaching in everyday practice

As we said in the chapter's introduction, we cannot create a definitive "when and when not to use Emotion Coaching" list. However, here we have collated research findings and the wisdom of practitioners working in community and educational settings to offer a series of insights to help you decide and guide your practice.

When using Emotion Coaching, it's important to remember the following points:

- Emotion Coaching is not a quick fix, a panacea that cures all ills, a substitute for specific interventions, or a therapy.

- Gottman and colleagues (1997) recognized that Emotion Coaching was not appropriate for all situations that parents find themselves in, and our research in community and educational settings corroborates. It is a given that the safety of the child and adult is of paramount importance and must never be compromised by any of our actions and deeds.

- There are times and situations when Emotion Coaching may not be applicable and as you practice Emotion Coaching you will come to know more about when it is, and is not, appropriate. From research (Gottman *et al.*, 1997; Rose, Gilbert and McGuire-Snieckus, 2015), it seems that Emotion Coaching can sometimes be less effective in certain contexts such as those listed below. However, this list does not mean that you cannot do Emotion Coaching in such situations, just that it may not work as effectively for different reasons. For example, you'll see having an audience is on the list below—for older children, receiving Emotion Coaching in front of their peers may not be productive. But we also know that observing Emotion Coaching in action can be an effective means for emotion socialization where children start to use it themselves, as seen in the examples in Chapter 1.

  Emotion Coaching may be less effective when:

  - large numbers of children are involved

  - there is an audience

  - you do not know the child

  - your approach is not sensitive to the developmental ability of the child

  - you are working with parents experiencing acute mental health issues

  - you are feeling anxious, distracted or too tired

  - you are pressed for time

- you believe the child is faking the emotions and is being manipulative

- you are inconsistent in your use.

- Whatever the age of the child, there remains a desire for an emotional connection with empathic, caring adults. However, how this is conveyed, and their needs will change as they grow. Being able to anticipate what issues are likely to be important to the individual child supports your understanding of their emotional needs. One practitioner told us, "You can't use it on teenagers" but came to understand that it was the way in which she was using it that showed why it wasn't working for her— she kept jumping too quickly to the problem-solving element, which they weren't always interested in discussing. She realized what they most wanted was empathy and validation, something which reflects the work of Katz and colleagues (2012).

- Young children have to learn to regulate the physiological arousal that results from social and emotional interactions, so they need opportunities to feel heightened emotions in order to practice and experience calming down (these opportunities will arise naturally). They need adults to anticipate and be sensitive to their moods, because it is through co-regulation that children learn to soothe themselves and self-regulate. They also need to know that it is possible to calm down after extreme emotions and, in this case, will especially rely on adults to interpret emotional cues. Remember that you can help a child feel more secure in themselves and their relationship to you by expressing and showing in your actions your understanding of their emotional thoughts and feelings.

- Fear is a natural emotion that serves a healthy function, and while children should not be fearful of exploring and learning, they do need to be appropriately cautious. The world can be a dangerous place. Emotion Coaching can help children to talk about their fears and develop strategies for coping with them.

- During middle childhood, children's cognitive ability develops in its complexity and they begin to learn how to manage their emotions through intellect and logic. In thinking for themselves, children begin to develop their own sense of values. They can be driven by a desire to fit in and tend to avoid anything that might draw attention to being different. They hone their skills in reading social cues, particularly if they want to avoid teasing and rejection, common threats at this age. Although most children develop these skills, children who have had Emotion Coaching from parents or carers master it most effectively because they have learned from an early age to do so (Gottman et al., 1997). Children more practiced in understanding social cues, and who respond appropriately and regulate their own emotions, have greater chances to avoid a public loss of control and potential humiliation.

- One of the advantages for children who have experienced Emotion Coaching is that their social skills are transferable and last well into adolescence. This is a time when children start to take more personal control, to define who they are and experiment with new identities and realities. By their teenage years, children have internalized the values of those around them and reap the benefits that come with emotional intelligence. Many teenagers do not want to be told what to do or how to solve problems, but they do want their emotional experiences to be accepted, validated and listened to empathically and without judgement. They are able to recognize when adult interest or apparent empathy is just another opportunity to lecture. Teenagers need to be supported to feel confident to make appropriate independent decisions, affirming that their choice matters. Children who have experienced Emotion

Coaching have many useful tools to know how to get along with friends, handle strong emotions, to manage and often avoid risks and have the confidence to cope with life's ups and downs. They have resilience.

- The adult–child relationship is not a democracy, as it is the adult or parent/carer who determines what behaviors are permissible. However, as Ginott (1972) advises, neither should it be a dictatorship. The role of the adult is not to provoke anxiety or arouse guilt, and those in authority need to be sensitive to their impact and effect on others. Children should be encouraged and feel empowered to have and practice choice, given that they have little control in their daily lives.

- It takes time to change old habits and develop Emotion Coaching relationships. You need to get to know a child and develop a mental map of their emotional world, which includes knowing about important people, places and events in their lives. In this way, you have a foundation on which to begin meaningful discussions and develop trusting relationships.

- Be open, honest and patient with the child and yourself. The goal in Emotion Coaching is to show the child, through your actions and words, that you see their emotional distress and empathize. Your response is to help them feel calm and open up a dialogue to problem-solve.

- The positive and preferred focus of survival is through social engagement. We all seek and respond to love, security, knowledge and understanding. Children want to show affection and be socially successful, know how to avoid dangers and be accepted. Emotion Coaching uses this natural preference to support children to experience and build skills that enhance their social engagement systems, allowing them to manage effectively the stress response system and optimize learning, health and wellbeing.

Getting started with Emotion Coaching

We have noticed some common queries and issues when people start to use Emotion Coaching, and so here we include a set of general tips for getting started with it. These have been developed by the North East England Emotion Coaching Practitioners and Mentors and are based on their experience of using Emotion Coaching in community and educational settings. We hope you find them useful.

Who shall I try this with?

- Do not try Emotion Coaching for the first time on your most tricky relationship. Give yourself an "easy win" and lots of opportunities to practice. Practicing the skills is essential.

- You need some success with Emotion Coaching, no matter how small, so that your confidence grows. You need to practice and reflect on the process, so it becomes "a way of being."

You get out what you put in!

- You have to do it, practise and "get it wrong!" It needs to become "second nature." The adult reflecting on the whole situation, including themselves, is central in the process. This skill itself takes time, lots of practice and encouragement.

- No matter how experienced you are, have humility and be kind to yourself. You won't always "get it right" or interpret the situation correctly. This is okay and is human. Compassion is called for in understanding the child/young person and in "reading between the lines" or beyond the "surface text." Self-compassion is also needed for you, the adult, in the situation.

This is not a "quick fix," you are building connections

- The Emotion Coaching process is just that, a process, and we are not looking for an immediate solution; this is a journey which we embark on with the child together, jointly. Emotion Coaching may begin as a technique or skill but at its best it becomes a way of being.

- Emotion Coaching takes time and there are no quick fixes, but every small step matters.

Do what is possible

- You don't need to do all of the Emotion Coaching steps immediately; however, Steps 1 and 2 are fundamental to supporting relational connection and emotional co-regulation. Sometimes the steps may be split across time, sometimes it is only possible or appropriate to go so far, which is fine. You need to apply it appropriately to the situation and the child/young person. This means knowing your child/young person well, and you may need to do lots of observation first—attune to the emotions.

- You do need to spend time on Steps 1 and 2, and don't jump too quickly to Step 3 (unless there are safety considerations) or Step 4, as you lose the opportunity for teaching and learning about emotions. Connect with the child.

- Ask yourself, "Has the child had an opportunity to learn or become more self-aware?"

- Remember why you are doing what you are doing, and what

Emotion Coaching is about. Read your notes, read books, seek out online resources and understand the principles and philosophy. Emotion Coaching isn't a means of behavioral control. It is a means of enhancing human connection, trust and relationships. Emotion Coaching is evidence-based practice, critically reflecting the latest research, and has a clear structure.

- Missing opportunities, or missing steps out, is normal in the development of your skills. Be kind to yourself and become more self-aware.

- Once you are very familiar with the process it becomes possible to adapt Emotion Coaching to different situations.

- Integrating Emotion Coaching into everyday practice happens in stages, through experiences and over time. Practitioners need to be aware of emotions; able to accept that emotions matter to learning; have opportunities to adopt and adapt it into their professional practice and be supported to sustain it through integration into policies and culture (see Figure 5.1) (Gilbert, 2018).

In the next chapter, we use the Emotion Coaching model of engagement (Gilbert, 2018) to explain how Emotion Coaching can be integrated into practice and different settings.

Chapter 5

Applying Emotion Coaching to Your Everyday Practice

> If you have a child in your class, or children within the school who are not emotionally stable, how are they going to learn? They can't, because there's too much rubbish flying around in their head, there's too much anger, there's too much angst; and so we need to be able to recognize it and to quickly deal with it, and I think this Emotion Coaching is brilliant for it.
>
> *Ruth, primary school teacher*

In this chapter, we describe your Emotion Coaching journey and how Emotion Coaching becomes integrated into your practice. Based on research into practitioners' experiences of using Emotion Coaching in everyday educational and community practice, we offer you a model that is a useful tool to help plan, monitor and evaluate your own Emotion Coaching journey.

Although this model may largely reference practitioner experience, it is, however, of equal relevance to parents and carers. Indeed, many practitioners are parents and carers and, although contexts may vary, Emotion Coaching journeys share similar pathways, and similar factors can help or hinder progression. Regardless of your role, we can assure you that the best way to gain skills and confidence in Emotion Coaching is simply through practicing it and sharing your experiences with others.

Emotion Coaching journeys

There are three factors that have been positively associated with children's social and emotional learning: classroom climate, including the development of high-quality trusting relationships; emotional socialization; and an adult's social and emotional competencies (Jenning and Greenberg, 2009).

Emotion Coaching not only makes explicit the connections between emotion regulation and behavior in children but also the knowledge and skills needed by adults to support these. Emotion Coaching is a universal relational approach, providing a guide on how to act and how to foster relationships effectively. When Emotion Coaching practice is replicated by other adults across a whole setting, the setting's emotional and communicative environment fosters and sustains calm, trust and learning. This in turn positively contributes to all the children's social and emotional learning.

What Emotion Coaching brings to community and educational settings

Before looking at the Emotion Coaching model in detail, here's a quick reminder of what Emotion Coaching offers you as an adult and the children and your setting.

- It is a simple and adaptable tool for practitioners and parents.

- It can be used to generate a community-wide, consistent approach to supporting all children's behavior.

- It provides a model for promoting empathic responses and thought constructions that support behavioral self-management in children.

- It provides practitioners and parents with an alternative relational model to support their work rather than the traditional behaviorist principles of sanctions and rewards.

- It promotes nurturing and emotionally supportive relationships, which can provide the best contexts for the promotion of resilience and sustainable futures (Gilbert, 2018, Rose *et al.*, 2015, Gus *et al.*, 2015).

How Emotion Coaching becomes part of your practice: starting your Emotion Coaching journey

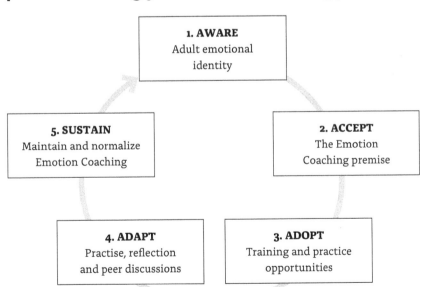

FIGURE 5.1 EMOTION COACHING MODEL OF ENGAGEMENT (© GILBERT, 2018)

The five-staged model in Figure 5.1 is informed by interviews with practitioners on their Emotion Coaching journeys. They discussed their training experiences, their frequency of use of Emotion Coaching and their reflections on both the process (i.e. using Emotion Coaching in settings) and the product (i.e. the outcomes for the child, themselves and others). It is a simplified version of the original model (Gilbert, 2018).

This cyclical and incremental model suggests that there are five key stages on any Emotion Coaching journey, and at each of these stages there are factors that can influence progression. As you journey, your accumulating Emotion Coaching experiences will contribute to and subsequently influence the next stage. However, whether Emotion Coaching becomes fully integrated, part of or perhaps a marginalized practice, the good news is that it raises adults' emotional awareness. This increase in emotional awareness contributes to and informs personal understanding. In turn, this can revise interest in and acceptance of the Emotion Coaching premise that "emotions matter to learning," providing further opportunity to revisit and reconsider Emotion Coaching in practice. And so, the cycle begins again, and their Emotion Coaching journey continues.

With the model in mind and thinking about your own Emotion Coaching journey, the next section will take a closer look at each of the stages.

What's happening at each of the model's stages?

Stage 1: Aware (emotional awareness)

This is the starting point of any Emotion Coaching journey. Every adult has an emotional identity which influences their awareness of emotions. Emotion identities are complex, reflecting a combination of the individual's meta-emotion philosophy, meta-cognition, personal self and professional self. The components of an emotional identity are not fixed and evolve as we age, therefore emotional identities can and do change (Gilbert, 2018).

As mentioned in Chapter 4, meta-emotion philosophy refers to your reactions, responses and reasoning about emotions in yourself and others (Gottman *et al.*, 1997). Meta-cognition reflects the beliefs held about the cognitive processes that best support and monitor learning. Finally, whether we see our personal and professional selves as the same or distinct influences perceptions and shapes responses to roles, rights and responsibilities, including relationships in our working lives. It is also worth remembering the contribution of statutory professional codes of conduct on preferred teaching styles and creative approaches to children and learning.

Therefore, emotional identities are important as they influence acceptance of the fundamental Emotion Coaching premise that "emotions matter to learning." This in turn impacts on attitude, engagement and energies to any Emotion Coaching training undertaken.

Emotional identities can be viewed as lying on a spectrum:

- At one end of the spectrum is "largely acknowledging of emotions."

  - For example, when discussing emotions and behaviors, Abdul said, "I automatically assume an emotion is a result of a behavior, or a behavior is a result of an emotion."

- At the other end of the spectrum is "mostly disapproving of emotions."

  - For example, Jen believed, "You can't bleat on about emotions all day; that's not the sort of person I am."

- And somewhere in between is "generally unknowing of emotions."

  - For example, Maya mused, "Although we are quite open and caring, I don't know that we do actually talk about our emotions very much."

Stage 2: Accept

This stage focuses on your response to the Emotion Coaching premise that "emotions matter to learning." Your emotional identity influences your level of acceptance of this statement, and to a degree, is also an indicator of your potential interest and commitment to Emotion Coaching. The combination of emotional identity and acceptance of the Emotion Coaching premise means that practitioners can be categorized as being:

- Emotion Coaching receptive (largely acknowledging of emotions).

  - For example, Paul believed emotions were important and that, "Your emotions impact on your behavior and, well, they lead your behavior, they go hand in hand."

- Emotion Coaching unreceptive (mostly disapproving of emotions).

  - For example, to support academic learning, Fran thought that schools should be rule and regulation driven. She summed this up as, "I see it as discipline versus emotion."

- Emotion Coaching undecided (generally unknowing of emotions).

  - For example, Lenni had not really thought about the role of emotions in education and stated, "Well, I've never really thought about emotions having a special purpose before."

Stage 3: Adopt

This stage relates to your Emotion Coaching training experience and subsequent opportunities to "have a go." Many factors influence the training experience, including:

- Your personal level of interest in Emotion Coaching.

- Whether you are learning alone and guided by resources that are self-selected or you are part of a group and directed by specialists.

- Whether attendance at Emotion Coaching training is voluntary or compulsory.

- The course content and delivery style (e.g. self-directed, outside trainers or in-house, interactive or lectures, includes relevant case studies, peer discussion and activities, take-away resources).

- Timetabling (e.g. specified and protected training time, in school or personal time, the availability of cover to attend all or only some of the training, duration and timing of the training: morning, afternoon or twilight).

- Chosen training venue and location (e.g. in house or away, and transport networks), other participants (e.g. whole setting, role specific or year teams).

- Refreshment provision and facilities (e.g. coffee breaks, refreshments, bring your own, space for eating/relaxing).

Factors such as these do play a part in motivation and subsequent commitment to having a go at doing Emotion Coaching in your setting.

Positive Emotion Coaching training experiences lead to greater confidence about your knowledge and understanding of emotions, behaviors and relationships. This helps you to feel better skilled and motivated to try Emotion Coaching in your setting. For example, Ray found that the training experience helped him to move from being undecided about Emotion Coaching to committing to Emotion Coaching, saying, "The training was helpful. I must admit I was a bit on the wall beforehand, and now I'm not quite on the wall. I'm sort of more positive than not positive." For some, Emotion Coaching training affirms their typical practice approach to teaching and learning, endorsing what they have always thought about emotions, behavior and learning. Mary's practice was relational based and attending Emotion Coaching training with her colleagues made her feel "almost vindicated about what I'd been doing, and I just thought, I have been doing the right thing all along."

However, with less favourable training experiences or if the Emotion Coaching premise challenges your emotional identity, you may be less enthusiastic to trial Emotion Coaching in practice. For example, Talia's training experience was compromised because teaching assistants in her setting attended the one-day training event but were unable to attend the following supporting Emotion Coaching workshops. This affected her commitment and motivation to try Emotion Coaching. She said, "When you went on the day training it was quite inspiring, it made you really want to do Emotion Coaching, but because we didn't have ongoing training, it went by the wayside a little bit."

Having plenty of opportunities to both practise and reflect with others about Emotion Coaching encourages its adoption into practice. For example, Penny felt very self-conscious at first, but being able to talk with others and seeing colleagues using it gave her the confidence to persevere, "It felt strange at first, trying to remember the steps, but I really found talking about how you could use these things and moving the model on was really useful." Hana agreed, "When you talk to each other and hear other people, how other people have dealt with different things, it makes you think 'Oh, that situation happened with us, and I didn't do that' and 'Oh, I've done those situations,' or 'That hasn't happened to me, but now I know that if it does, what to do.'"

For Jane, the frequency of Emotion Coaching use was key to feeling more skilled and confident, "The more I used Emotion Coaching, the easier it was to do and the less I needed to think about it. It means now I just sort of do it and it just happens." Finally, Sunni suggested that having the opportunity to talk together as staff about Emotion Coaching was particularly helpful for those who were struggling, "For those people right at the other end of the spectrum, it is like making those discussions come up, so maybe it is making them think more about Emotion Coaching as well."

As a result of the frequent references made by practitioners to the benefits of practising Emotion Coaching and sharing ideas and understanding with others, we coined the Emotion Coaching UK mantra: "You need to practise to improve practice."

Stage 4: Adapt

Positive outcomes from managing emotional incidents increases your Emotion Coaching skill base and encourages further use. Emotion Coaching can then move from being reserved for specific incidents with certain children to being applicable to a wider audience. Emotion Coaching use with mostly encouraging outcomes increases confidence to adapt Emotion Coaching and integrate it with other everyday practices. For example, because Emotion Coaching was complementary to many of the approaches Renal already used, she combined it with them, enhancing her practice repertoire, "We do restorative conversations here, and Emotion Coaching works. It fits beautifully into what I do and think." Renal was a deputy head of a primary school and believed that it was Emotion Coaching's adaptability that made it particularly useful. She believed that Emotion Coaching could be used successfully by many different practitioners, in a variety of ways, for many different situations. This was important "because even if everyone in the school uses Emotion Coaching, they use it to different degrees depending on what's going on with the child. I would not expect to see identical plans because you are different people to your year group partner, and your class are completely different."

Stage 5: Sustain

This stage is about normalizing Emotion Coaching in everyday practice, whether you choose to use it as your "go to" to manage specific emotional incidents or it informs your whole practice approach and becomes "just what you do." Emotion Coaching practice reflects the combination of your Emotion Coaching training experience, personal commitment and practice; however, to be sustained it also requires commitment and support from managerial and peer networks.

Factors that help to both normalize and sustain Emotion Coaching in your practice include the following:

- As mentioned earlier, it really helps if there are others who have trained and are also using Emotion Coaching. Our studies have shown that adopting "a whole-setting approach" to training helps integration and normalization of Emotion Coaching into practice and, indeed, into a setting's culture. For Sally, having whole-setting training meant there was a shared staff understanding and acceptance of Emotion Coaching, "Because they've all been on the training, it didn't sound woolly to them, it made sense." Alice believed that whole-setting training was important as it clearly promoted Emotion Coaching as the preferred setting's approach, "I think it was useful that you had all aspects, you had the teachers, the caretaker, the dinner lady, everybody doing it, so no one person could say they couldn't do it or didn't know how to do it." Liam suggested that whole-staff training helped the children as there would be a more consistent response from all staff. Reliable and predictable responses help children to understand the rules and relationships and be able to focus their energies on learning, "Well, you're all on the same page, aren't you? It's consistent: it's consistent with helping, it's consistent with our policies, it's consistent with how the child's feeling, and then it goes back to happy child, happy learning, doesn't it?"

Whole-setting training experiences can give practitioners "a sense of belonging" to their setting. For example, Jeza, a teaching assistant, felt he was more willing to listen and participate in trialing Emotion Coaching because all the staff had trained together, "I'll listen to you because we've done this together. I don't think Emotion Coaching would have been so much to the fore had it just been the teaching assistants doing it, because there wouldn't have been that level of involvement."

- Having opportunities to see colleagues in your setting use Emotion Coaching boosts your confidence and understanding and encourages peer discussion about teaching practices. Diana noted that since the whole-setting training there was more general discussion about professional practice and enthusiasm to share practice tips in the staff room, "Emotion Coaching has been seen as a whole-school thing and, I think we've been talking about it more, as a staff, between us." Dan thought that having whole-setting training had led to a greater tolerance of differing teaching practices, "We can all talk about Emotion

Coaching because we're all aware, we can talk about how we deal with the parents in the group and dealing with difficult situations, from that emotional point of view."

- Appointing identifiable Emotion Coaching lead practitioners means these adults can act as focal points for staff post-training and help to sustain interest. They can keep Emotion Coaching on the setting's agenda, act as role models and motivators for colleagues and help coordinate the continuing training needs of the setting.

- Commitment and engagement of managerial staff is critical to sustain Emotion Coaching practice. Cathy, a deputy head of a large secondary school, believed that for Emotion Coaching to become successfully integrated into practice, management must provide adequate resources and be seen to be actively involved and participating. She noted that it was "very important when we're doing anything new with staff that they see that it goes all the way through, and that we're doing the same thing." Another practitioner with managerial responsibility commented on the advantage of evidencing senior involvement from the start of any Emotion Coaching project, "Because it was embedded in management and senior staff, it was easier to sell to the rest of the staff and the cover supervisors and teaching assistants."

- All the policies and procedures that inform the setting's infrastructure and culture can be adapted to include reference to Emotion Coaching commitment. These include, for example, revising the behavior management policy to become the behavior regulation policy; renaming time-out/exclusion facilities to reflect a focus on emotional regulation support; developing rolling Emotion Coaching training programs and a refresher program for all staff; including Emotion Coaching as a routine agenda item at staff meetings; referencing Emotion Coaching in specialist child support plans and professional development supervisions; sharing Emotion Coaching with parents and carers.

Returning to Stage 1: Aware

As a result of your Emotion Coaching training experience you will have raised emotional awareness. Your current Emotion Coaching journey can confirm, inform or challenge your reactions to emotions and learning, and in doing so modify your emotional identity. Therefore, your Emotion Coaching experience itself creates further opportunities to review the Emotion Coaching premise, and the Emotion Coaching model of engagement starts again and so you continue on your Emotion Coaching journey.

An example of an Emotion Coaching journey was recounted by Fiona, a secondary school teacher and year head. Acknowledging that the Emotion Coaching premise had challenged her emotional identity, she believed she started her Emotion Coaching journey as "emotionally dismissive" and "Emotion Coaching unreceptive." However, using the approach resulted in her feeling more in control and effective as a practitioner and created better outcomes and engagement with children. She felt that she had become more aware of emotions in herself and others, more approachable and a better practitioner:

> *Fiona was sceptical of the need for Emotion Coaching in schools. She saw schools as needing to be rule-driven places to prioritize academic learning. Although she believed she was emotionally aware and empathetic, she felt Emotion Coaching appeared rather "wishy-washy" and unnecessary. However, the school adopted a whole-school approach to training. Having time to reflect helped her realize communication was bi-directional, "You suddenly think that some really difficult*

situations have been caused by me not using Emotion Coaching and by me being tired and grumpy." She was surprised at how successful Emotion Coaching was with children and how it helped to improve her everyday relationships with them. Emotion Coaching "really enabled me to connect with them in a way that I haven't quite done before." As a result of the positive effects, she increased her Emotion Coaching usage to include a greater variety of situations, and with different children and parents. As a practitioner, she believed she was now calmer, and more in control of her own emotions as well, "I don't get angry as much, I don't get frustrated as much because the children aren't getting as angry and as frustrated." Additionally, Fiona was "feeling more competent about expressing what I think, acknowledging certain feelings in my own life—this is new to me." She had noticed that "if you use it properly it teaches you a little bit about your own emotional state as well."

Reflecting on her pre- and post-training practice, Fiona commented, "When I first came, my end game for the children in particular situations who are outside the classroom or whatever, or kicking off, was to get them to do what I wanted them to do, so get them back in, and get them learning, and that is still the end game. But that isn't my overriding aim. My overriding aim now is to get them calm and get them into a position in which we can look at what is actually best for them at that moment. So, it's taking myself out of the equation and actually just centering on what is best for them." Her practice was now more child focused, "Emotion Coaching gives children a sense that there's someone in school who understands and who they can trust." She recognized that her use of Emotion Coaching had changed, "Before, I was kind of at the end of my tether and didn't know what else to do, whereas now it's my first port of call." Emotion Coaching was now her common practice, "I'm flexible with how I use it in different situations, but I think the fundamentals of it have been great and surprising."

Using Emotion Coaching in your practice—a spectrum of use

Emotion Coaching may be your natural approach to teaching and learning, but if it isn't it can be learned. As Helen suggested, "You have to be a certain type of person to be able to feel Emotion Coaching, but you can evolve to be that type of person." Emotion Coaching is simply a relational rather than a behaviorist approach which allows you to work with rather than on children, as Mel said, "Don't do 'to' children, but do 'with' children."

The diagram below summarizes what practitioners have told us about how they use Emotion Coaching in their practice. Although Emotion Coaching use varies between individual practitioners, it can be seen as positioned on a continuum. On the Emotion Coaching Practice Continuum at one end Emotion Coaching is used as "a technique" and at the other as "an approach" (Gilbert, 2018).

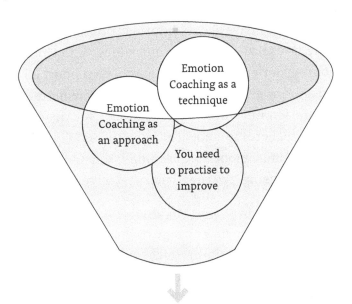

"Emotion Coaching is a way of being and a way of becoming"

FIGURE 5.2 THE EMOTION COACHING SPECTRUM OF USE

Emotion Coaching can be a technique to manage emotional incidents in your everyday practice as well as an approach that underpins teaching and learning in your practice and settings. Let's look at these in a bit more detail:

- *Emotion Coaching as a technique* to manage specific emotional incidents. Ruth, a lunchtime supervisor, used Emotion Coaching to manage children's squabbles in the playground, "It's amazing what just a turn of phrase will do, and I come back to that, and I am still consistently surprised at that recognition for a child and enabling them to label that emotion. I think is the most powerful thing you can do." Kara saw Emotion Coaching as a simple, flexible tool, "It's a communication tool, isn't it, with other adults, as equally as it is with children?"

- *Emotion Coaching as an approach.* Emotion Coaching is integral and informs your teaching practice approach (indeed, Emotion Coaching may have always informed your practice!). Through frequent use and positive outcomes, Emotion Coaching becomes your everyday teaching tool to support all children's learning. For example, Toya reflected, "The more and more I use Emotion Coaching, and the more I see the outcome, the more it will become embedded as a process." Lola believed, "It's just how I am... Emotion Coaching is a listening approach, as opposed to being 'I'm the authority, you're not.'"

- *Emotion Coaching as a technique and an approach.* Your use of Emotion Coaching may change over time to reflect your experience and needs. Karime thought about her Emotion Coaching journey and believed, "Emotion Coaching maybe starts out as a technique but then actually it just becomes natural, so Emotion Coaching develops into your natural approach." Interestingly, for practitioners new to education or to the ideas informing Emotion Coaching practice, Emotion Coaching is often initially used as a practice technique to manage specific emotional incidents or when other, more familiar, methods have failed. Positive outcomes increase confidence so that over time the applicability of Emotion Coaching becomes less focused and more generalized.

We coined the phrase "Emotion Coaching is a way of being, a way of becoming" because your emotional identity, training experience and setting environment influence and are influenced by your Emotion Coaching practice. This was summed up by a manager of an early years setting who, having implemented Emotion Coaching as a whole-school approach, simply stated, "Emotion Coaching is what we do. It's the way we are."

However, changes in emotional awareness and effects of Emotion Coaching on your practice are not always easy to monitor. As Maggi noted, "Because Emotion Coaching evolves you don't notice it, do you? But when you reflect back you think, oh, actually yes." Having time to think about your own Emotion Coaching journey—where you started, what's happened on the way, and where you are now—is invaluable, as are opportunities to reflect with colleagues. David, a trainee teacher, reckoned, "Emotion Coaching is something that becomes a way of life over time and I'm still falling into that one, I'm still understanding that."

Challenges you may encounter on your Emotion Coaching journey

If you are new to the idea of Emotion Coaching or Emotion Coaching is new to your practice, it helps to be aware of potential pitfalls. Although you may encounter challenges on your Emotion Coaching journey, that's normal, you are not alone, and most can be resolved.

Before we discuss how to manage possible difficulties you may encounter, it's important to remember, as we mentioned in Chapter 4, that Emotion Coaching is not the answer to all problems for all children and, indeed, there are times when it is not appropriate. However, it is a successful, evidence-based, relational approach that can help you to support children to manage their emotions and to develop self-regulation skills (Gottman *et al.*, 1997; Rose, Gilbert and McGuire-Snieckus, 2015; Gus *et al.*, 2015).

The Emotion Coaching model of engagement discussed earlier in this chapter is a flexible tool that you can use to guide and monitor your Emotion Coaching journey. Each of the stages can be viewed as separate but they are also incremental, in that progress at each stage is informed by the previous stage's outcomes. It is the interaction between who you are, what you as a practitioner bring and your Emotion Coaching journey that influences the adoption, adaption and integration of Emotion Coaching.

To sustain Emotion Coaching in practice you need:

- a willingness to learn and a commitment to adopt

- time to use, reflect and adapt

- monitoring to be sustained.

Let's now take a quick look at each of these in turn to find out more about potential challenges.

Willingness to learn and commitment to adopt

If you are a practitioner who is "mostly disapproving of emotions" or unreceptive to the premise "emotions matter to learning," your Emotion Coaching training experience may be challenging. Ruth recognized the difficulties some staff had to fully engage with Emotion Coaching, "I think it does depend sometimes a little bit on the person's character and how comfortable they are with emotions and maybe themselves...so that it might be a little bit harder to get on board with it." Nesta agreed and thought practitioners who did not voluntarily attend Emotion Coaching training struggled because they were less committed, which then compromised their engagement in learning about and trialing Emotion Coaching. She believed, "Some of them are doing it by rote, they're not doing it from the heart."

Some practitioners said that although they used Emotion Coaching in their professional practice with children and as parents, they were less comfortable using it with colleagues. They felt that Emotion Coaching had been introduced to them as a teaching tool to manage children and emotionally charged situations. Therefore, if used with co-workers it could be misinterpreted as manipulative and patronizing. Caitlin, a manager of an early years center, found Emotion Coaching supportive of her setting's culture, but was concerned about a potential conflict arising for some practitioners taking Emotion Coaching training as personal criticism, "It's okay to teach your staff and send them on courses to up their maths skills, but when you're saying 'Let's make you an Emotion Coaching practitioner,' it's almost taken as criticism, like, 'I'm okay, so why do I need to do this?' So it's a step that I think needs to be done, but it's a scary step." She advocated the importance of allaying fears by offering whole-setting Emotion Coaching staff training and providing clear ongoing managerial support from the outset.

Therefore, consideration needs to be given to who is attending, their emotional identities and an acceptance that Emotion Coaching is a journey not just a destination.

Time to do, reflect and adapt

Feeling "time poor" was the most frequently cited obstacle to dealing with emotions. Toya believed she had always overlooked emotions because "there's never enough hours in the day, always so much work to be done, people are so busy doing stuff that you forget about what's going on inside." Jack worried about the ever-increasing conflicting demands of his role, "Is it my job to emotionally develop these children, to a certain extent yes, but actually primarily it's also my job to be able to teach these children to read, to write, to be able to add, subtract."

To effectively support integration and sustain Emotion Coaching, management need to be involved and be prepared to provide practitioners with both the time and resources needed, "Emotion Coaching is really simple, so obvious, but not when you don't have time out to think about things." As a result, Kathy proposed that to sustain Emotion Coaching, "it needs to be revisited and re-talked about, and I think maybe in tutor teams doing Emotion Coaching, certainly with learning directors taking a leading role."

Emotion Coaching both creates and benefits from having established, mutually trusting relationships with a child. However, relationships take time to develop and need opportunities to flourish, as Caitlin noted, "You can use Emotion Coaching whenever, and sometimes you will see benefits and sometimes you won't see benefits... I think it does depend on the relationship with the children that you've got. Children have to find the right person for them to talk to." Fiona acknowledged that she felt that there were particular children who were "completely uninterested in school... and because they're not interested, they're not interested in what I think about them."

Nesta believed that some children did not respond to Emotion Coaching because their home life had not given them the appropriate life skills. Although we stress that Emotion Coaching is not a "cure all," there is plenty of evidence to justify ongoing use. It is true that you may not initially sense or see the response you had hoped for in a child. However, understanding about how we learn (Chapter 1) we know that experiencing consistent, empathic responses from adults supports emotional self-regulation and, over time, builds trusting adult–child relationships. Through your co-regulation, the child can experience, copy and develop their own skills of self-regulation.

Monitor to sustain Emotion Coaching

When proposing to introduce any new way of working or practice, such as Emotion Coaching, you want to be able to measure impact. Therefore, planning and monitoring are necessary. As a universal, relational approach, Emotion Coaching is not subject or year-group specific, therefore it is more difficult to monitor using routine measures. Primary school practitioner Nikki was appointed Emotion Coaching Lead for her setting and wondered, "How do we police it in effect, you know, how do we make sure that people are using it and what do we do when people really aren't using it?" Toya managed an early years setting and questioned, "Everyone needs to know this, but how am I going to embed this, how am I going to roll it out... How to get the key message across to an audience that's going to be varied?"

The model can be used as a planning and assessment tool as each of the stages have specific identifiable factors that influence outcomes. The sequential stages (Aware, Accept, Adopt, Adapt, Sustain) can be used to construct a strategic plan for effective Emotion Coaching implementation. Combining routinely collected institutional data with case studies focusing on incidents of use and responses of children can provide outcome-based evaluations to monitor change and look at improving behavioral outcomes.

In summary, the table below shows the model and factors for consideration at each of the stages.

TABLE 5.3 FACTORS INFLUENCING THE MODEL OF ENGAGEMENT (©GILBERT, 2018)

Emotion Coaching cycle	Emotion Coaching stage	Emotion Coaching stage focus	Factors that can influence Emotion Coaching stage outcome
	1. Aware	Practitioner's emotional identity	Practitioners have differing "emotional identities" which influence their interest in Emotion Coaching. Emotional identities reflect: an awareness of emotions, including reactions, responses and reasonings about emotions in ourselves and others (i.e. meta-emotion philosophy); beliefs about the role of education in learning and thinking (i.e. metacognition) and beliefs in emotional roles, rights and responsibilities as a practitioner and as an individual (including relationships). Practitioners can be described as being: "largely acknowledging of emotions," "mostly disapproving of emotions," or "generally unknowing of emotions."
	2. Accept	The Emotion Coaching premise	The statement that informs Emotion Coaching training is "Emotions matter to learning." As a result of emotional identity and response to the Emotion Coaching premise, practitioners can be categorized as 'Emotion Coaching receptive," "Emotion Coaching unreceptive" or "Emotion Coaching undecided."
	3. Adopt	Emotion Coaching training intervention and Emotion Coaching practice	Practitioner training experience can be largely positive or negative. The efficacy of Emotion Coaching practice reflects recruitment style, training experience (delivery and content), appointment of setting-based Emotion Coaching leads (to coordinate and motivate), peer support and opportunities to practise.

4. Adapt	Ongoing Emotion Coaching practice, reflection and peer discussion	Ongoing practice within settings; regular opportunities for shared peer reflection; ongoing support and informal teaching; effective peer role models support adaption of Emotion Coaching into everyday practice repertoires.
5. Sustain	Emotion Coaching maintenance	Managerial engagement and support (time and finance) throughout the project; appointment of Emotion Coaching leads in setting; ongoing formal and informal training opportunities (including integration into new staff induction package); Emotion Coaching consideration/integration into setting policies; evaluation of Emotion Coaching practice using pre-existing setting data sources and practitioner case studies; diversification of Emotion Coaching training opportunities e.g. for parents/carers, governors and peer mentoring projects.

Your Emotion Coaching journey: where are you now?

We know that with peer support and practice (with largely positive outcomes) Emotion Coaching moves from being a novel, specific intervention to one that has broader applicability to other areas of practice. For some practitioners, the changes are minor, but confidence increases. Others may initially be cautious, needing time to practice Emotion Coaching, but as they become more confident, it becomes increasingly integrated into their everyday practice. For a few practitioners, Emotion Coaching is transformational in changing their practice and emotional identities.

Having read this chapter and perhaps having chatted with others, you may find you are all at different stages in your Emotion Coaching journeys. So, where are you right now?

Perhaps you:

- *are a reluctant traveler.* Jess was such a practitioner. She struggled to accept the Emotion Coaching premise "emotions matter to learning," believing that schools should focus on a child's academic ability and leave emotions to the parents. However, as a result of her Emotion Coaching training experience she now acknowledged that "I can see how Emotion Coaching can work, but I still just struggle with the whole lot of it...even if I don't agree with Emotion Coaching, it's not saying I wouldn't do it... I think it would be in the back of my mind if it needed to come up, but Emotion Coaching wouldn't be a tool I'd use." Interestingly, Jess went on to add that, in her role as a mum, she had used Emotion Coaching and found it helped her remain calm and resolve problems quicker!

- *now realize you want to be a traveler.* Bea had been largely unaware of emotions and rather unsure about the Emotion Coaching premise, so could be labeled as "Emotion Coaching undecided" at the start of her Emotion Coaching journey. Having trained in and then used Emotion Coaching she recalled being surprised and pleased that Emotion Coaching had worked with the children. This encouraged her to use it again and again, "I was made to eat my words, seeing Emotion Coaching in action, wholly and truly. It's been fantastic."

- *are new to traveling but now well on your way*. Fiona had found that the training experience initially challenged her understanding of her professional role and the role of emotions in learning. However, as she practised Emotion Coaching, she noticed changes in her understanding of the relationship between emotions, behavior and learning. This was then reflected in her approach and her relationships with the children, "Emotion Coaching seems a soft approach at the beginning, but I think everyone needs to remember that the fundamental aim of this approach is to get the kids to do the right thing... I don't shy away from saying that there are consequences to actions that are wrong—you have to do this—but it's just enabling them to be in a frame of mind to be able to acknowledge that."

- *are an experienced and seasoned traveler*. Cathy felt that her Emotion Coaching training experience both affirmed and validated her established practice approach. Emotion Coaching provided her with opportunities to reflect on and "fine tune" her normal practice approach. She noted, "It turns out Emotion Coaching is what I've been doing all along, it's what I do. I don't know whether I've got to grips with it all yet. I am in the process of thinking about it...and I don't know whether that will ever stop actually."

For more information and support on using Emotion Coaching in your practice, check out the tips, written by practitioners for practitioners, in Chapter 4.

We will leave the final words about Emotion Coaching to Chloe, who declared, "It's not just a load of old gobbledy-gook you know, and it's not just one of those buzz words for the moment and something else will come along. I don't think it will, I think it has a huge place in schools."

Chapter 6

Supporting Strategies

This chapter makes links to tools and strategies that you might want to use, or are already using, to support children's social, emotional and behavioral development. These include theoretical frameworks that complement or reflect the Emotion Coaching approach, such as attachment theory. Complementary strategies can enhance your use of Emotion Coaching and help you to see how it fits in with the other ways you support children's development. References to other theories and strategies are briefly summarized to illustrate their synergy with the particular steps of Emotion Coaching. These links are not exhaustive but refer to strategies or theories that have been utilized or applied in case studies from our research.

Links with calming strategies and related theories (Steps 1 and 2 of Emotion Coaching)

As we know, sometimes we need to deal with and support children who have effectively "flipped their lid" and are dysregulated. Their behaviors are largely driven by the stress response system, as outlined in Chapter 1. We also saw, in Chapter 3, how using lots of language and trying to engage in problem-solving before calming the child invariably is ineffective.

Attuning yourself to the intensity of emotions the child is feeling—often through noticing their physical response—can help you decide which activities may help to soothe and calm the child's emotional state. The aim is to support them to become sufficiently calm so that you can start to engage in the more language-based aspects of Emotion Coaching. Thinking about how you can help a child to calm the autonomic part of the brain through co-regulation is the key here. With an increasing number of calming strategies being used in schools that draw on theories of sensory integration, self-regulation and attachment theory, your knowledge of the child is useful to recognize their calming preferences. These engage a more holistic approach and often focus on how to help the body to calm and put the "lid" back on. The calming strategies mentioned below are useful practical tools to add to your toolkit and have been successfully used alongside the more language-based tool of Emotion Coaching.

Physical calming activities

You might encourage a child to do some of these activities:

- Do some deep breathing with you. Breathing out for a longer period than breathing in stimulates the vagus nerve, which, as we read about in Chapter 1, is involved in calming the body from a stressed emotional state. Ask the child to focus on pushing out their tummy as they fill their lungs as this will help to draw in the air. There are many ways to help children to do this, depending on their age. For example, with younger children you can ask them to imagine they have a balloon in their tummy that they need to blow up and then let deflate. Other children might be able to imagine a butterfly gently spreading out its wings inside so they need to push out their tummy and lungs to make space, then they can imagine the butterfly slowly flying out. This is especially helpful for those children who feel "butterflies" in their tummies whenever stressed. We have also found that asking the child to imagine blowing out candles on each finger a useful way to encourage calmer breathing.

- Engage in progressive relaxation. This shifts a child's attention to their physical state and by relaxing clenched muscles, allows the automatic part of the brain to understand that the body no longer needs to be in fight/flight mode. Focusing on a physical sensation, such as something they can see, something they can hear, or something they can touch, may help, but success can depend on how calm they are at the start.

- Encourage the child to walk, run, sway or rock with you. Rhythmic repetitive movement can trigger the vagus nerve to help settle the nervous system. Pushing and pulling activity can also help a child to dissipate the energy generated by the stress response to support fight/flight behaviors.

- Suck on ice cubes, or suck water or yoghurt through a straw. These activities make use of the sucking reflex, which is calming for many children.

Calming spaces

The creation of a "calming" or "peace" corner has also become increasingly popular with many of the schools and parents with whom we have worked. These are designated areas in the classroom or home, equipped with comfortable seating and various sensory-based materials, such as fidget toys, colouring books, mini-massagers, bubbles, smelling bottles, body socks, bubble wrap and kaleidoscopes. They are designed to provide a safe space where children can go to feel calm with you or by themselves. In Chapter 2, we heard about the three-year-old who sat in a "calming chair" to help him calm down from a tantrum. The team also put other sensory objects nearby, which he could use to help himself feel calmer. He quickly found some favourites—a squeeze ball, a drum to bang, and a gloop jar—which helped him to calm down while the adult nearby made soothing noises and used Emotion Coaching.

Some of these activities draw on the research of Stuart Shanker (2016) whose work on self-regulation fits very well with Emotion Coaching, reflecting much of the material covered in Chapter 1 of this book. He draws on research about how the brain and body stress system operates and how stress affects children's behavior. He also emphasizes the importance of relationships in self-regulation and learning. He points out that children can have differing stressors within the differing aspects of their lives, each of which may trigger a stress response. This calls on adults to be "stress detectives" and co-regulate a child within their various domains, helping them to identify each stressor and learn how to manage them. He too warns against getting "too meta-cognitive" before the child is ready to engage with cognitive thinking when distressed. Again, this theory correlates with Emotion Coaching which encourages adults to view a child holistically as they learn self-regulation.

The idea of calming spaces and particularly breathing exercises links well with the practice of mindfulness which is becoming increasingly used within schools in the UK. Based on the work of Kabat-Zinn (2006), mindfulness invariably involves mindful breathing exercises which can help you feel calmer and more in control. During one research project, a teacher introduced it to her class of 10- and 11-year-olds, along with Emotion Coaching, to support them in their forthcoming SATs (standard assessment tests). She observed some children using the techniques during their SATs. Afterwards, the children expressed how they had used

Emotion Coaching to recognize their feelings and mindfulness breathing exercises to help calm them when they encountered a tricky problem. We revisit this idea at the end of this chapter.

Sensory integration

Although the research base for the effectiveness of sensory-based materials and activities is still under-developed, the ideas reflect the work of theorists such as Ayres (1972) who has worked on sensory integration. Sensory integration is based on a growing understanding of how our brain and body organize sensory information and how the way we process and integrate sensory input affects our feelings and behavior. This is helpful in understanding why sensory-based materials can help soothe and calm a child. The materials or activities appear to work with the child's sensory and stress response system, soothing their nervous system and facilitating them to feel more comfortable and secure. They help to generate an optimal level of arousal and regulation which supports children to function and behave more effectively, ready to engage in learning (Lane *et al.*, 2019).

Our own research (Rose *et al.*, 2019) has shown how sensory materials can be integral in assisting a child to calm their stress response system, not just for children with sensory processing difficulties, but for any child. One child on the autism spectrum found playing with a Rubik's cube helped to soothe his anxiety and, along with Emotion Coaching, enabled him to engage in useful discussions to moderate his behavior. He thought that the predictable, rhythmic movement and visual stimulation of the cube helped him to feel safe. Some other examples from our research show that combining different strategies, particularly to help children calm down, can be most effective. In Chapter 3, Maria made use of calming sensory activities with Sam, as they sucked cold water through a straw, popped bubble wrap and clenched and released a stress ball. Maria had paid careful attention to Sam's physical state and understood the benefits of taking time to calm and soothe Sam's sensitive and highly aroused state.

Attachment-based specialist interventions

The way in which physical materials can help a child to feel safe is also seen in a primary school that created a wall of plaster prints of all the children's hands. This was quite a feat, but in times of stress, each pupil could press their hands into their own prints and the sensations of pushing against the wall and of feeling their hands being enclosed by their own prints helped to generate a soothing effect. This idea of feeling safe and secure is based on attachment theory, which was discussed briefly in Chapter 4 (Bowlby, 1988).

Emotion Coaching can complement other strategies that draw on attachment theory such as Theraplay® and Nurture Groups, both specialist interventions facilitated by trained practitioners. Theraplay® was developed by Jernberg (Booth and Jernberg, 2010) and is used to support trauma, emotional dysregulation and behavioral difficulties. Nurture Groups are group-based interventions that focus on supporting children with social, emotional and behavioral difficulties (Bennathan and Boxall, 1998).

Taken from our research, here is an example of Theraplay®, Nurture Group and Emotion Coaching being used together to support an eight-year-old boy whose behavior was so challenging that he required two support assistants to be present at all times:

> *The combination of attachment-based strategies had a significant effect, with Emotion Coaching being used in the everyday interactions and the specialist interventions being used for targeted work with the child. Each strategy was cited by the child, the family and the practitioners as playing a part in helping to increase the child's attendance and eliminating the need for exclusions while also*

increasing academic engagement. As a result of the improvements in behavior, only one teaching assistant was required to support him. When asked about Emotion Coaching, the child declared, "I feel I can talk to my teachers, they listen, and it stops the volcano in my tummy."

The use of Emotion Coaching to support children who have experienced trauma needs to be carefully considered and applied sensitively. Nonetheless, our research has revealed numerous examples where it has been used effectively with children who have experienced trauma (Rose, Gilbert and McGuire-Snieckus, 2015; Rose *et al.*, 2017; Rose *et al.*, 2019). For example, two foster families who were trained in Emotion Coaching reported on the way it had transformed their relationship with the children they were fostering. One involved a three-year-old and another a 14-year-old, both of whom had experienced significant trauma and had numerous difficulties with their ability to self-regulate, often leading to conflict. Both families changed from focusing on the behavior and started connecting with the children emotionally. As one remarked, "It made a difference almost immediately." Changing the way they communicated with the children triggered a cascade of positive outcomes, including improved behavior and wellbeing for all concerned, even the foster parents. Review reports, written by the children's social workers to document the foster placement developments, recorded that they were "astounded" by the progress made by each child.

Preparing children for upcoming emotional challenges

The steps of Emotion Coaching can be used in a preventative way, prior to a potentially challenging event. Adults anticipate how a pupil or group of pupils might feel about a future situation, and then prepare them for this by using pre-emptive Emotion Coaching:

1. Anticipate what the children might feel in a forthcoming situation.

2. Label those feelings, maybe commenting on the physical response the children might expect, and explain, or consider, why they might be feeling like that.

3. Remind children of the expectations for behavior.

4. Help the children to come up with suitable strategies.

For example, Dan, a teacher of children aged seven to eight years, was aware that his class became very excited during assemblies, particularly those to which parents and carers were invited:

> The day before the assembly, Dan spoke with the class about feeling excited by the assembly, and the fact that, with some of their parents being there, they would maybe feel "over-excited." Dan and the class talked about what behaviors they display when they feel very excited: talking, giggling, laughing, waving arms about and maybe accidentally hitting or banging into others. Dan and the children considered how this might look to the parents and reflected on whether this was the way they wanted their parents to see them at this important assembly. The class then came up with ideas of what they could do to help themselves calm down when they noticed themselves becoming over-excited. Dan and the class had been regularly practicing deep breathing as a regulatory strategy and the class thought that this might be a practical strategy for the assembly. And so, they had a short practice session. Dan reported that he was pleasantly surprised at how well the assembly had gone and how calm and in control the children had been.

Ryan, a headteacher in a primary specialist social, emotional and mental health provision, prepared for a school trip where he anticipated that Tom would find some of the arrangements anxiety provoking and frustrating:

> *Ryan prepared Tom for the trip by saying, "Tom, I know that normally you like to sit at the front of the bus, but this time you won't be able to and will need to sit on the third row from the front. You might find this annoying and it might make you feel cross and a bit angry. In the past when you've felt like this, you have tried to push others out of the front seat." Ryan explained that it was okay to prefer to have a particular seat, but that could not always be the case, and this time Tom would not be able to have his preference. They discussed what to do to help Tom deal with the situation and agreed that listening to his favourite music once he was in his seat would help him stay calm. On the day of the trip, Tom was able to get to his seat on the bus without incident and enjoy the whole experience.*

In many ways, this idea of anticipation and preparation of the emotions is similar to Social Stories (Gray, 1995). Social Stories are mini-books which contain short descriptions of a particular event or activity, helping a child to understand specific instructions or information about what to expect in that situation and why. This pre-emptive Emotion Coaching, anticipating and preparing for an expected emotion, makes the emotional content of the event more explicit, allowing the children to "rehearse" their feelings and how they might manage the situation.

Links with limit-setting and problem-solving strategies (Steps 3 and 4 of Emotion Coaching)

A range of more formal problem-solving frameworks or complementary approaches have been utilized as part of Emotion Coaching in Step 4. What follows is by no means an exhaustive list. Remember that problem-solving forms only part of Emotion

Coaching, which has the initial interpersonal attuned connection at its core.

Cognitive behavioral (CB) approaches

The problem-solving aspect of CB-type methods fits in neatly with Emotion Coaching. The CB framework can be seen as a more structured approach to Step 4—the exploration and sharing of ideas to agree a solution, as described in Chapter 3.

A child could be asked to consider what they were trying to achieve with a particular behavior, what was done to achieve that goal and what was the resulting outcome. The child could then be asked to try and come up with other options to achieve that goal and then for each way to try and think what the outcome might be. The FRIENDS programme (Barrett, Lowry-Webster and Turner, 2000) uses this helpful problem-solving model:

1. What is the problem? After you have followed through on consequences for inappropriate behavior, find out what was the goal the young person was trying to reach with that behavior.

2. What could I do? Ask the child to come up with several possible solutions to the problem. Don't shoot down suggestions even if they are not workable.

3. List what might happen for each solution. You can help them by asking is this fair, will this work, is it safe? How are you likely to feel? How are others likely to feel?

4. Pick the best solution. If the child comes up with an unworkable solution, it's okay to go forward with it as long as it's harmless. Leave the door open to rethink the solution if it doesn't seem to be working. You can help the young person to come up with a plan of action to accomplish the solution.

5. Do it.

6. Did it work? What went well and what might you do differently next time?

Solution-focused approaches

Solution-focused approaches come from the work of De Shazer (1982) and have been translated successfully into school settings (Kelly *et al.*, 2008). They work well as part of Step 4 in Emotion Coaching and can be used as an alternative to CB problem-solving approaches. This is because, sometimes, continually focusing on a problem can turn you into an expert on "what's wrong" but perhaps doesn't translate very well to becoming expert in knowing "how to fix it." Solution-focused approaches acknowledge this issue, and place attention not on what needs fixing, but on what is working well for the child and what has worked well in the past. Adults can help children focus on a preferred future, perhaps by thinking of a way they would like to behave, and helping to identify when they have previously displayed attributes of being successful in a similar situation. The child can then be supported to come up with a plan to show these behaviors more often and to try the next step along the path to the desired state.

Some of the conversations you have with a child in a solution-focused manner could include:

- How did you avoid getting really aggressive when you felt angry?

- What stopped complete disaster from occurring when you made a mistake?

- Tell me about times when you don't get angry.

- Tell me about times you have felt the happiest.

- When was the last time that you feel you had a better day?

- What was it about that day that made it a better day?

- How have you managed so far to stay calm when he/she says those things that annoy you?

- What is working to help you get your work done in science?

Scaling questions and their follow-ups can help children to see some of the successes and positives that have been happening.

- On a scale of 1–10, with 10 representing the best it can be and one the worst, where would you say you are today?

- (A follow-up question) Why did you give a four and not a five?

Restorative conversations

We discussed in Chapter 3 children's need for "repair," to make things better when a relationship has "ruptured" and broken down. Restorative conversations are a component of restorative practices which emphasize the restoration of good relationships when there has been conflict or harm. McCluskey and colleagues (2008) have adapted this approach for use in educational contexts, and the restorative-based problem-solving in Step 4 of Emotion Coaching might help a child make steps towards repair. A simple restorative conversation might include the following steps:

1. What happened?

2. Who was affected?

3. What were you feeling? (You may need to use Emotion Coaching to support the child with this step.)

4. What were the others involved feeling?

5. How can we make things right?

An important point underpinning individual restorative conversations and in the wider sense for schools or organizations engaged in restorative practices, is that there presupposes an ability of the child to understand what they are feeling and what others are feeling. Without these skills, a child will not be able to successfully engage in restorative conversations. With scaffolding (i.e. the four steps of Emotion Coaching), an adult can support a child to develop an understanding of their own emotions and those of others.

Zones of Regulation

The Zones of Regulation (Kuypers, 2011) is a framework that uses four colours (blue, green, orange and red) to help students identify their feelings and level of alertness, and it provides strategies to support emotional regulation. By understanding how to notice their own body's signals, detect triggers, read social contexts and consider how their behaviors impact those around them, students learn improved emotional control, sensory regulation, self-awareness, and problem-solving skills.

One school linked the colours of the Zones of Regulation with the steps of Emotion Coaching to help school staff talk to children about what they were experiencing, why this was occurring and what they might do about it.

Emotional intelligence

Emotional intelligence (Goleman, 2007) refers to our ability to recognize, understand and manage our own emotions as well as recognize, understand and influence the emotions of others—emotional literacy has been similarly described. It's clear how this relates to Emotion Coaching. In the UK, many schools have emotional literacy activities, such as circle time to talk about feelings, a worry monster to "post" their worries, worksheets focusing on developing a sense of self and self-esteem, activities which engage children in recognizing different emotional states, and worksheets that encourage reflection on triggers and strategies for managing emotions. These all fit well with the use of Emotion Coaching.

Paying attention to and enhancing the good

Chapter 1 mentions the basic emotions we are all born with, and that we have an in-built bias towards experiencing difficult emotions which has evolved to ensure our survival. As a result, although we prefer to learn through our social engagement system, our survival instinct means that negative stimuli get more attention, negative interactions are more powerful than positive ones and we have the capacity to readily experience these regardless of our age. We generally learn faster from pain than pleasure; people work harder to avoid a loss than attain an equal gain; it is easier to create learned helplessness than it is to undo it.

The earlier part of the book also discussed neuroplasticity. Neuroplasticity is stimulated by what we pay attention to, therefore directing attention skilfully—the essence of mindfulness—is an important way to shape the brain.

A strategy making use of neuroplasticity to support the development of emotional regulation is to help children pay attention to the positive and so sensitize the brain to positive experiences. Hanson (2013) formulated the acronym HEAL to aid focus on the good:

1. **H**ave a positive experience. Notice or create it.

2. **E**nrich the experience through duration, intensity, multimodality, novelty, personal relevance.

3. **A**bsorb the experience by acknowledging it and feeling that is sinking into you as you sink into it.

4. **L**ink positive and negative experiences (this is optional—when you are feeling calm and secure you could give thought to an experience which caused you to feel angry).

We can help children to engage in attention-shifting focusing activities, such as deep breathing and progressive relaxation, and pay attention to the effect these have on the body and their emotions. Activities such as shared journaling allow children to pay attention to the positive in the day. Asking children to note down things they are grateful for or giving them opportunities to do things for others are all ways in which we can help children pay closer attention to the good. They help support emotional regulation and enable children to learn positive prosocial behavior. Many of these ideas link closely to positive psychology (Seligman and Csikszentmihalyi, 2000) which engages with thoughts, feelings and behaviors that focus on strengths.

Conclusion of the book

Now that we have reached the end of the book, we thought we'd leave you with a quote which reminds us of the role emotions play in our lives and how Emotion Coaching can play a pivotal role in supporting our ability to self-regulate, promote positive behavior and contribute to our resilience and wellbeing in the classroom and beyond: "Emotions are the glue and the gunpowder of human social relations" (Oatley and Johnson-Laird, 2014, p.138). Emotion Coaching makes the glue stronger and the gunpowder less explosive.

We wish you all the best with your Emotion Coaching journey.

Glossary

Attunement: The process of attuning to children's needs. In Emotion Coaching it is about tuning in to what the child might be feeling, and fostering a sense of being seen and feeling safe. In moments of distress, an attuned relationship between an adult and child can influence and organize the mind of the child and enable the child to regulate themselves in the moment, to develop their regulatory capacity and acquire skills for use in the future.

Behavioral approach: Refers to strategies used to manage behavior, such as rewards and sanctions. It considers that development is essentially the result of external stimuli and focuses on the modification of behavior through the use of positive and negative reinforcement techniques.

Co-regulation: Involves working with another person to help them regulate their feelings and behavior. It involves warm, responsive interactions which provide support, coaching and modeling to help others understand, express and regulate their feelings, behavior and thoughts. Emotion Coaching is a co-regulating strategy as it operates like a scaffold that supports another by helping them to learn to calm down, by providing a narrative to help them learn about their own emotions and how they can be regulated more effectively, leading to self-regulation.

Disapproving style: One of the parenting styles identified by Gottman and colleagues (1997), which involves no empathy but lots of guidance. Disapproving parents also tend to ignore or dismiss the child's feelings, viewing them as weak or manipulative or unproductive, and instead focus on the behavior which needs to be controlled via punishment or other means. Emotional displays are judged or criticized.

Dismissing style: Another parenting style identified by Gottman and colleagues (1997), involving little or no empathy and no guidance. Dismissing parents tend to ignore or minimize a child's emotions, viewing them as trivial or unimportant. They tend to rely on logic, distraction or reward to help a child feel better rather than engaging with emotions which they fear may prolong the emotional state.

Emotional identity: Emotional identities are complex, reflecting a combination of an adult's meta-emotion philosophy, meta-cognition, personal self and professional self. Everyone has an emotional identity which reflects their awareness of emotions and acceptance of emotions in themselves and others. Emotional identities are not fixed and as we age, emotional identities can and do change.

Emotion Coaching: A way of communicating with a child who is struggling to manage their emotions in order to help them to learn to regulate their feelings and behavior. It is about helping children to understand the different emotions they experience, why they occur, and how to handle them. It focuses attention on the feelings which are driving the behavior, not just the behavior itself, and involves a process of recognizing, empathizing, validating and labeling feelings, setting limits on behavior if needed, and problem-solving solutions for more effective ways of regulating feelings. It was originally coined by Gottman and colleagues (1997) to reflect the way in which parents respond to and support children's emotions.

Emotion Coaching model of engagement: An evidence-based, cyclical and incremental model which suggests that there are five key stages on any Emotion Coaching journey (Aware, Accept, Adopt, Adapt, Sustain). At each of these stages, there are factors that can influence progression and contribute to the following stage. It is informed by research with Emotion Coaching practitioners/adults who discussed both the process (i.e. using Emotion Coaching in settings) and the product (i.e. the outcomes for the child, themselves and others). It is a simplified version of the original model (Gilbert, 2018).

Emotion Coaching premise: In order for Emotion Coaching to be integrated effectively into practice, the adults in the educational setting need to accept the premise that "emotions matter to learning."

Emotion Coaching receptive: Being largely accepting of the Emotion Coaching premise that "emotions matter to learning." Emotional identity is considered to be "largely acknowledging of emotions."

Emotion Coaching style: The parenting style Gottman and his colleagues (1997) found to be the most productive in terms of positive outcomes for children. It embraces both empathy and guidance. All emotions are recognized, accepted and validated. Emotional displays are an opportunity to listen, empathize, label and offer guidance on boundaries, where needed. It is about teaching socially appropriate behavior and problem-solving skills and helping children to learn to self-regulate.

Empathy: The ability to understand and share the feelings of another. In Emotion Coaching terms, it involves the ability to recognize, label and validate a child's emotions. Affective, or emotional empathy is being able to share a feeling in another through an emotional connection. Cognitive empathy relates to our ability to understand how another might be feeling and thinking. Compassionate empathy involves having a desire to take action to help support another.

Internal working models: A theory which considers that we all have stored memories of early interactions with caregivers which eventually become "event scripts" of beliefs and expectations, and serve as a generalized interpretation of, a child's and others' actions and behaviors. They are essentially mental representations to help us understand the world, ourselves and others, thus guiding our interactions with others.

Laissez-faire style: The least common parenting style identified by Gottman and colleagues (1997) involves empathy but no guidance. Laissez-faire parents tend to accept a child's emotions, believing that children need to release their emotions, but do not attempt to help regulate their children through limit-setting or problem-solving.

Mentalizing/mind mindedness: Separate but similar terms linked to the attunement process. Both refer to the way in which a parent treats a child as if they have their own thoughts and feelings. They involve actively accepting the child has their own mind and then attuning to the child in order to help understand their needs, desires, feelings and interests.

Meta-emotion philosophy: Our knowledge of reactions, responses and reasoning about emotions in ourselves and others. Although there are recognizable types of meta-emotion, everyone's meta-emotion is unique, and is known as their meta-emotion philosophy. It affects awareness of emotions, awareness and acceptance of emotions in a child, and how we coach a child about the emotions.

Mirroring: Our natural ability to learn through watching and copying others. We appear to have brain mechanisms involving neural networks that support our understanding of the actions of others and also help us to also interpret their intention. Modeling Emotion Coaching appears to play an important role in supporting its impact.

Relational approach: Strategies used to help children learn to manage their own behavior through a relationship and way of interacting that embodies core values such as respect, compassion and inclusiveness. One such strategy is Emotion Coaching. A relational approach recognizes the fundamental role that relationships play in human development and that such development is holistic. The focus is on helping the child to learn self-regulation through co-regulation support of positive behaviors.

Self-regulation: The ability to manage stress levels, emotions, behavior and attention so that we're able to achieve goals and engage in learning, behave in socially acceptable ways and maintain good relationships. Self-regulatory skills help children to have conscious control in managing their emotions, behaviors and thoughts, particularly disruptive and impulsive ones, despite the challenges and unpredictability of the world around them.

Social engagement system: A term coined by Porges (2011), it is part of our survival system and is a complex system within our brains and linked to our body which focuses on communication and connecting with others to help our survival. According to Porges, it works with our survival system to manage our emotional and behavioral responses.

Stress response system: A complex system in our brain which is linked to our body, involving different neuronal connections, organs and neurochemicals that work together to help us survive by triggering survival behaviors to help protect us. It manifests largely in fight, flight and freeze responses.

Vagal tone: (in this book) A person's ability to regulate their stress response so as to be able to engage appropriately within the social world. Vagal tone is in part genetic, but also reflects brain maturation and environmental, experiential and relational experiences. Emotion Coaching is associated with good vagal tone.

References

Ahmed, S. (2018) *Developing an Attachment Aware Behavior Regulation Policy: A Relationship Based Approach to Inclusion*. Brighton: Brighton and Hove Inclusion Support Service.

Ayres, A.J. (1972) *Sensory Integration and Learning Disorders*. Los Angeles, CA: Western Psychological Services.

Baron-Cohen, S. (2011) *The Science of Evil: On Empathy and the Origins of Cruelty*. London: Basic Books.

Barrett, P., Lowry-Webster, H. and Turner, C. (2000) *FRIENDS Program for Children: Participants Workbook*. Brisbane: Australian Academic Press.

Baumeister, R. and Vohs, K. (eds) (2004) *Handbook of Self-Regulation: Research, Theory, and Applications*. New York, NY: Guilford Press.

Bennathan, M. and Boxall, M. (1998) *The Boxall Profile Handbook for Teachers*. Maidstone: Association of Workers for Children with Emotional and Behavioural Difficulties.

Booth, P. and Jernberg, A. (2010) *Theraplay: Helping Parents and Children Build Better Relationships Through Attachment-Based Play*. San Francisco, CA: Jossey-Bass.

Bowlby, J. (1988) *A Secure Base: Parent-Child Attachment and Healthy Human Development*. London: Routledge.

Cozolino, L. (2014) *The Neuroscience of Human Relationships*. New York, NY: Norton.

De Shazer, S. (1982) *Patterns of Brief Family Therapy: An Ecosystemic Approach*. Guildford: Guilford Press.

Duckworth, A.L. and Seligman, M.E. (2005) "Self-discipline outdoes IQ in predicting academic performance of adolescents." *Psychological Science*, 16(12), 939–944.

Durlak, J., Weissberg, R., Dymnicki, A., Taylor, R. and Schellinger, K. (2011) "The impact of enhancing students' social and emotional learning, a meta-analysis of school-based universal interventions." *Child Development*, 82(1), 405–432.

Ekman, P. (2016) "What scientists who study emotion agree about." *Perspectives on Psychological Science*, 11(1), 31–34.

Feinstein, L. (2015) *Social and Emotional Learning: Skills for Life and Work*. London: Early Intervention Foundation.

Fonagy, P., Gergely, G., Jurist, E. and Target, M. (2004) *Affect Regulation, Mentalization and the Development of the Self*. London: Karnac.

Fonagy, P. and Target, M. (1998) "Mentalization and the changing aims of child psychoanalysis." *Psychoanalytic Dialogues*, 8(1), 87–114.

Gilbert, L. (2018) *Introducing Emotion Coaching into Primary, Secondary and Early Years Educational Settings: The Voice of Practitioners and Model of Engagement*. School of Science, Bath Spa University. Accessed on 17/10/2020 at http://researchspace.bathspa.ac.uk/11551.

Gilbert, L., Rose, J., Palmer, S. and Fuller, M. (2013) "Active engagement, emotional impact and changes in practice arising from a residential field trip." *International Journal of Early Years Education*, 21(1), 22–38.

Ginott, H. (1972) *Teacher and Child*. New York, NY: Avon Books.

Golding, K. (2015) "Connection before correction: Supporting parents to meet the challenges of parenting children who have been traumatised within their early parenting environments." *Children Australia*, 40(2), 152–159.

Goleman, D. (2007) *Emotional Intelligence: Why It Can Matter More Than IQ*. New York, NY: Bantam Books.

Gottman, J. and DeClaire, J. (1997) *Raising an Emotionally Intelligent Child: The Heart of Parenting*. New York, NY: Simon and Schuster Paperbacks.

Gottman, J., Katz, L. and Hooven, C. (1996) "Parental meta-emotion philosophy and the emotional life of families: Theoretical models and preliminary data." *Journal of Family Psychology*, 10(3), 243–268.

Gottman, J., Katz, L. and Hooven, C. (1997) *Meta-Emotion: How Families Communicate Emotionally*. New York, NY: Psychology Press.

Gray, C. (1995) *Social Stories and Comic Strip Conversations: Unique Methods to Improve Social Understanding*. Jenison, MI: Jenison Public Schools.

Gross, J. (2015) "Emotional regulation, current status and future prospects." *Psychological Inquiry*, 26, 1–26.

Gus, L. (2018a) *Supporting Adults to Develop Emotion Coaching in Schools*. Kingsbury Schools Together Emotion Coaching Training Project Evaluation Report.

Gus, L. (2018b) "Mental Health and Emotional Wellbeing in the Early Years." Keynote Speech, The Future of Early Years Conference, Salford, 2018.

Gus, L., Rose, J. and Gilbert, L. (2015) "Emotion Coaching: A universal strategy for supporting and promoting sustainable emotional and behavioral well-being." *Journal of Educational and Child Psychology*, 32(1), 31–41.

Gus, L., Rose, J., Gilbert, L. and Kilby, R. (2017) "The introduction of Emotion Coaching as a whole school approach in a primary specialist social emotional and mental health setting: Positive outcomes for all." *The Open Family Studies Journal*, 9, 95–110.

Gus, L. and Woods, F. (2017) "Emotion Coaching." In D. Colley and P. Cooper (eds) *Emotional Development and Attachment in the Classroom: Theory and Practice for Students and Teachers*. London: Jessica Kingsley Publishers.

Hanson, R. (2013) *Hardwiring Happiness: The Practical Science of Reshaping Your Brain and Your Life*. New York, NY: Random House.

Havighurst, S., Wilson, K., Harley, A. and Prior, M. (2009) "Tuning in to kids: An emotion-focused parenting program-initial findings from a community trial." *Journal of Community Psychology*, 37(8), 1008–1023.

Immordino-Yang, H. and Damasio, A. (2007) "We feel therefore we learn. The relevance of affective and social neuroscience to education." *Mind, Brain and Education*, 1(1), 3–10.

Jenning, P. and Greenberg, M. (2009) "The prosocial classroom: Teacher social and emotional competence in relation to child and classroom outcomes." *Review of Educational Research*, 79(1), 491–525.

Kabat-Zinn, J. (2006) "Mindfulness-based interventions in context: Past, present, and future." *Clinical Psychology: Science and Practice*, 10, 144–156.

Katz, L.F., Maliken, A.C. and Stettler, N.M. (2012) "Parental metaemotion philosophy: A review of research and theoretical framework." *Child Development Perspectives*, 6(4), 417–422.

Kelly, M.S., Kim, J.S. and Franklin, C. (2008) *Solution Focused Brief Therapy in Schools: A 360 Degree View of Research and Practice*. Oxford: Oxford University Press.

Kuypers, L. (2011) *The Zones of Regulation*. San Jose, CA: Think Social Publishing.

Lane, S., Mailloux, Z., Schoen, S., Bundy, A. *et al.* (2019) "Neural foundations of Ayres Sensory Integration®." *Brian Sciences*, 9(7), 153.

LePage, J-F and Theoret, H. (2007) "The mirror neuron system: Grasping others' actions from birth?" *Developmental Science*, 10(5), 513–523.

Lieberman, M.D. (2013) *Social: Why our Brains are Wired to Connect*. Oxford: Oxford University Press.

McCluskey, G., Lloyd, G., Kane, J., Riddell, S., Stead, J. and Weedon, E. (2008) "Can restorative practices in schools make a difference?" *Educational Review*, 60(4), 405–417.

Meins, E., Fernyhough, C., Fradley, E. and Tuckey, M. (2001) "Rethinking maternal sensitivity: Mothers' comments on infants' mental processes predict security of attachment at 12 months." *Journal of Child Psychology and Psychiatry*, 42, 637–648.

Oatley, K. and Johnson-Laird, P. (2014) "Cognitive approaches to emotions." *Trends in Cognitive Sciences*, 18(3), 134–140.

Parker, R., Rose, J. and Gilbert, L. (2016) "Attachment Aware Schools – An Alternative to the Behaviorist Paradigm." In N. Noddings and H. Lees (eds) *The International Handbook of Alternative Education*. London: Palgrave.

Porges, S. (2011) *The Polyvagal Theory: Neurophysiological Foundations of Emotions, Attachment, Communication, and Self-Regulation*. New York, NY: Norton.

Porges, S. (2015) "Making the world safe for our children, down-regulating defence and up-regulating social engagement to optimize the human experience." *Children Australia*, 40(2), 114–123.

Porges, S. (2016) *Co-regulation*. Accessed on 17/10/2020 at https://www.relation-alimplicit.com.

Riley, P. (2010) *Attachment Theory and the Teacher-Pupil Relationship*. London: Routledge.

Rose, J., Gilbert, L., Gus, L., McGuire-Snieckus, R., McInnes, K. and Digby, R. (2017) "Attachment aware schools: Working with families to enhance parental engagement and home-school relationships." *Family Studies Journal*, 9, 160–171.

Rose, J., Gilbert, L. and Richards, V. (2015) *Health and Wellbeing in Early Childhood*. London: Sage.

Rose, J., McGuire-Snieckus, R. and Gilbert, L. (2015) "Emotion Coaching: A strategy for promoting behavioral self-regulation in children and young people in schools: A pilot study." *European Journal of Social and Behavioral Sciences*, 13, 1766–1790.

Rose, J., McGuire-Snieckus, R. and Gilbert, L. (2019) "Attachment aware schools: The impact of a targeted and collaborative intervention." *International Journal of Pastoral Care and Education*, 37(2), 162–184.

Schore, A. (2000) "Attachment and the regulation of the right brain." *Attachment and Human Development*, 2(1), 23–47.

Seligman, M. and Csikszentmihalyi, M. (2000) "Positive psychology: An introduction." *American Psychologist*, 55(1), 5–14.

Shanker, S. (2016) *Self-Reg: How to Help Your Child (And You) Break the Stress Cycle and Successfully Engage with Life*. London: Penguin Books.

Shonkoff, J. and Garner, A. (2012) "The lifelong effects of early childhood adversity and toxic stress, technical report." *American Academy of Pediatrics*. Accessed on 17/10/2020 at http://pediatrics.aappublications.org/content/pediatrics/early/2011/12/21/peds.2011-2663.full.pdf.

Siegel, D. (2012) *The Developing Mind: How Relationships and the Brain Interact to Shape Who We Are*. New York, NY: Guilford Press.

Siegel, D. and Payne Bryson, T. (2012) *The Whole-Brain Child*. London: Constable and Robinson.

Skinner, B.F. (1953) *Science and Human Behavior*. New York, NY: Macmillan.

Sroufe, A. (1995) *Emotional Development*. Cambridge: Cambridge University Press.

Sroufe, A. and Siegel, D. (2011) *The Verdict Is In: The Case for Attachment Theory*. Accessed on 17/10/2020 at http://www.fullyhuman.co.uk/wp-content/uploads/2020/05/Soufe_Siegel_Attachment-article-1.pdf.

Tronick, E. (1998) "Dyadically expanded states of consciousness and the process of therapeutic change." *Infant Mental Health Journal*, 19(3), 290–299.

Van der Kolk, B. (2014) *The Body Keeps the Score: Mind, Brain and Body in the Transformation of Trauma*. London: Penguin.

Winnicott, D.W. (1953) "Transitional objects and transitional phenomena: A study of the first not-me possession." *The International Journal of Psychoanalysis*, 34, 89–97.

Index